THE HEARTBREAK MENDER

GEORGE PANTAGES

Copyright © 2018

The Heartbreak Mender

By George Pantages

Printed in the United States of America

ISBN 978-0-9989538-2-3

All rights reserved solely by the authors. The authors guarantee all contents are original and do not infringe upon the legal rights of any other person or work. No part of this book may be reproduced in any form without the permission of the authors.

Unless stated otherwise, all Scripture references come from the NKJV translation of the Bible, copyright © 2006 Thomas Nelson.

KJV. Copyright © 2006 by Thomas Nelson.

George Pantages Ministries

Cell 512 785-6324
geopanjr@yahoo.com
Georgepantages.com

TABLE OF CONTENTS

Chapter 1
George Pantages
Why Me? 13

Chapter 2
Missti Jones
I was a child prostitute.. 29

Chapter 3
Dalila Janos
I didn't get to say goodbye to my husband............................. 43

Chapter 4
Jennifer Brown
I died, but my mama's prayer brought me back 61

Chapter 5
John Moore
My 16-year-old son died of cancer 75

Chapter 6
Sarai Jimenez
My daughter died in my womb and Jesus brought her back .. 95

Chapter 7
Adiel Sandoval
I was unjustly deported from the U.S..................................... 111

Chapter 8
Anthony Martinez
Childhood heartbreak caused my anger and bitterness 121

Chapter 9
Daisy & Edgar Arias
My wife was killed in an auto accident
and was sent back from heaven 135

DEDICATION

When I decided to leave my football career to pursue a life dedicated to Christ, I initially believed I had made a grave mistake. How so? All my endeavors to be pleasing in the sight of God fell by the wayside and I continually found myself falling short in whatever I attempted in Him. This is when I met a man of God by the name of Freddy Clark.

Attending one of his "Gifts of the Spirit" seminars was truly a life changing experience for me. First of all, the three-day seminar was FREE. We were offered lodging for FREE and were fed one meal a day also for FREE. This unselfish man of God was willing to share his knowledge and experience at no cost to the attendees, and this truly had a great impact on my life.

As time has gone on, I have followed in his footsteps very closely, yet my gifting is a little bit different because my focus is more on the emotional and spiritual healing of an individual. I remember him warning me if I truly would allow God to use me in the miraculous, I would be highly criticized and perhaps even ostracized. Although his words have rung true, it has not been enough to stop me from dealing with the BROKEN HEARTED.

I have now been doing this type of ministry long enough to enter into a mentoring stage. As I attempt to pass along to a new generation what Brother Clark has passed on to me, there is an excitement knowing that these new recruits will be used even more powerfully in the end times than I ever could be. Thank you, Bro. Clark for the great impact you have had on my life.

I LOVE YOU BROTHER FREDDY IN JESUS NAME!!!

Evangelist Freddy Clark

Old Fashion Tent Revivals

INTRODUCTION

Webster's dictionary defines heartbreak as experiencing crushing grief, anguish, or distress. Anyone who has had their heart broken can attest to the fact it is one of the most grievous emotions to overcome. It can have such a devastating effect that many people when in a situation that they must take a chance on love again, have to make a decision whether or not they will do it wholeheartedly. Recovering from heartbreak is not an easy thing to do. There are some folks that never recover from heartbreak and thus live their lives in shambles.

If only heartbreak could ultimately be avoided with the possibility of still loving someone without reservation. The risks involved are many, ones that many people will not venture out to experience again. *It's just too painful!* On top of that, it is staggering to believe the Lord would permit such devastation in the heart of one of His children.

Yet, in reality heartbreak is not done to you but rather for you. It really doesn't make any sense until you realize that it was heartbreak that allowed the Lord to give His life on Calvary. Heartbreak in our lives identifies us with Him and after the mending process, allows us to minister unto the heart broken in a more effective manner. The Lord is not willing to put on us anything that He himself did not go through. If heartbreak prepared Him to suffer a most painful death, then we must take the same attitude when it comes our way to realize He permits it to make us better in Him.

Let these testimonies talk to your heart and soul. Allow them to permeate the deepest depths of your being. Ask the Lord to give you a new understanding of heartbreak so you too can be more like Jesus.

APPRECIATION

I would like to take the time to appreciate the following people for their contribution on the publication of this book:

    Michelle Levigne – Editor
    Mlevigne.com

    Luis Villegas – Book Cover Design
    DPIXO Graphics, Dpixo.com

    Adiel Sandoval – Spanish Translation

    Maria Pantages – Typesetting

Your professionalism and expertise rang true throughout the entire process, making my writing a whole lot better than it really is.

 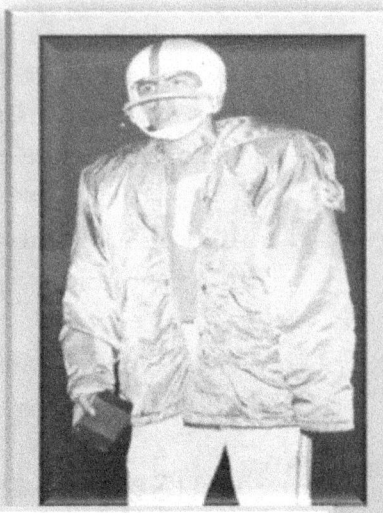

(1970) All So. Cal. P.A.T. record holder (55 in a row)

YESTERDAY'S HIGH SCHOOL HEROES
WHERE THEY ARE
ALL-CIF 4-A CLASS OF '71

Name-High School	Position	College	Status
Dennis Littlejohn, N. Torrance	TE	USC	Varsity baseball
Jim Lucas, Arcadia	SE	USC	Second-string safety
Terry Albritton, Nwprt. Hrbr.	T	Stanford	Shotputter
Todd Anderson, Buena	T	Stanford	Starter
Paul Charlton, Western	G	Cypress JC	Starter
Jim Samaduroff, El Rancho	T	Rio Hondo JC	Starter
Ken Lavigne, Santa Fe	C	Rio Hondo JC	Starter
Brian Longuevan, Rosemead	LB	Utah State	Starter
George Chance, Bishop Amat	LB	UC Riverside	Second-string safety
Kevin Bruce, St. Francis	LB	USC	Second-string
John Sciarra, Bishop Amat	QB	UCLA	Starter
Jeff Siemens, Westminster	QB	Stanford	Redshirt
Dan Larson, Alhambra	QB	(Pitcher in St. Louis Cardinals farm system)	
George Bennett, Pasadena	RB	Oregon	Third-string
Jamie Quirk, St. Paul	QB	(Shortstop in Kansas City Royals farm system)	
Joe Baumgaertner, Damien	RB	Stanford	Fourth-string safety
George Pantages, El Rancho	K	Rio Hondo JC	Did not play

Los Angeles Times – Sports (1972)

CHAPTER 1

George Pantages

I am not much of a Winter Olympics fan because I find the Summer Olympics far more interesting and exciting. But, there is one Winter Olympics that captured my attention somewhat unexpectedly. Not so much for the events being held, but rather some extracurricular activity that caught everyone off guard. Ice Skater Nancy Kerrigan, the odds-on favorite to win Olympic gold, was brutally attacked and severely injured during the '94 Olympic trials. It was speculated that her archrival, Tonya Harding hired someone to injure her enough so she could not compete in the Olympic Games. She had just finished a routine practice when someone, out of nowhere, whacked her on the leg with a pipe and she fell hopelessly writhing in pain. As she violently hit the ground, she began to shriek in utter despair, repeating the word, "why?" Luckily for her the injury was not career-ending and she healed up in time for the Olympics. Sad to say, Nancy never regained her form before the injury, and had to settle for the silver metal (2nd place).

"Why" moments are common in everyone's lives. There is no avoiding the question, although at times there does not appear to be any answers that will console the person asking. There have been so many "why me?" moments in my life that it appears sometimes they outnumber the experiences that can be explained. They began in my life at such a tender age, as far back as five years old when I suffered with polio. Because I was so young, I don't think I truly understood how close to death I came. I was placed in a quarantined two-bed room. Almost daily when waking up in the morning, I had a new roommate. Every once in a while, when I would ask what happened to Johnny or Mary or whoever else was sharing my room, I was always told they were just sent to another room. Unbeknownst to me, that other room was the morgue. They had died the night before! After the Lord miraculously healed me, I was transferred from General Hospital in Los Angeles to Rancho Los Amigos hospital in Downey for my rehabilitation. The only thing I remember about that place was the eerie feeling I would experience when everything would quiet down at night. Why could I not go home? Why was I feeling so afraid? As difficult as it was to adjust to physical limitations in my entire body, it was nothing compared to the verbal harshness inflicted on me.

When my first grade teacher saw me for the first time, she was aghast at my appearance. Under my shirt I wore a body cast that covered me from my chest to my waist. I was the original "Ninja Turtle." There were braces on both hands and arms, attached to thick wires that were then hooked onto the body cast. I was a sight to behold. I also wore orthopedic shoes, which I could not tie by myself. And I knew that I was going to need a whole lot of help. My teacher immediately went to the principal's office after school and demanded that the principal send me somewhere else. In those days, handicapped children were mainstreamed and there were no special ed classes for us, at least not in our school. When news of my teacher's opposition to teach me was brought to my mom's attention, she was livid. She proceeded to give my teacher a piece of her mind and this tongue lashing did not stop there. The principal of the school also received a portion of my mom's ire. When the dust settled, I was able to stay put and I excelled academically. A few years later in fourth grade, I had her as a teacher again but boy were things really different. I became one of the best students and after I entered high school and started doing really well, every year she would dedicate a section of her bulletin boards to post all of my newspaper clippings during my high school career.

But, she was not the only teacher with insensitive statements. There was one day in PE class in fifth grade, our regular teacher was absent. As everyone lined up for calisthenics, of course I had permission to stand there because most of the exercises I could not do. About five minutes into the calisthenics, the substitute teacher barked at me for all to hear. "What's the matter son, are you crippled?" In those days (1965) there was a great respect for authority and we would never disrespect our teachers. I wanted so badly to explain to him my situation, but something inside me said just take it. It was the longest PE session in my entire life. We were then dismissed back to our classes for the last half hour of school. I was holding back tears as much as I could, but when that last dismissal bell rang, I literally ran more than a mile without stopping till I got home. I remember running into my room and slamming the door behind me. I could not hold back my emotions anymore, sobbing uncontrollably. I remember asking God, "Why did you let me live? Why didn't you just let me die like the other children in the hospital, it would have been so much easier." Of course, the Lord did not answer and every once in a while, my "why" questions would pop up, but the end result was always the same, no response from God.

    Children can be just as cruel as adults, if not more so. As I got older, the braces on my arms and the body cast were no longer needed. The right side of my upper body was more affected by the polio than any other. I would walk with my right hand palm up. A few of the kids in the school, after noticing my twisted hand, had nicknamed me "Finger." The name was given because it appeared that I was always giving somebody the "middle finger" and it always brought a lot of laughs, to my embarrassment, of course.

My mom's ultra-positive outlook helped me to brush off pretty much any and all criticism that came my way. She would help me do sit ups, and during the process she always encouraged me to do my best because I was just as good as anybody else, if not more so. I actually believed her, and I joined the band in fourth grade, although I had to hold the trumpet backwards (playing the valves with the left hand and holding the trumpet with the right). That did not stop me from becoming the best trumpet player in the entire district by the next year. In the district concert held every year, I played a solo, for which I was given a rousing ovation. I honestly believe the applause was more for my effort as a handicapped person than my playing ability. Every good thing I did was always magnified to a great thing.

My self-esteem skyrocketed, so much so that I felt I had the confidence to do anything I put my mind to. My next challenge was playing sports. Of course, because of the handicap I was somewhat limited in what sport and what position I could play. I decided to try tackle football, knowing that the only position I would ever be able to play was a place kicker. I was good enough to make the varsity football team in my sophomore year (I was the only sophomore), was all Southern California in my junior and senior years, and I broke a Southern California kicking record that stood for sixteen years. I was well on my way to win a football scholarship at the University of Southern California (USC) when another "why me?" moment surfaced.

The Lord had been dealing with me, knowing that up to that point in my life I had not repented of my sins so that I might live for Him. To complicate things further, He was a distant second in my life, because in those years playing football was the most important thing to me. I came so close to ignoring His call and to this day it is difficult to fathom that I loved something more than I loved Him. He made it plain and simple when He used a favorite gospel song of mine that my sisters and I used to sing together, entitled, "Lovest Thou Me More Than These?" The lyrics taken from St. John 21:15-17 raced through my heart and mind while I was driving home from USC one day, and with tears in my eyes I answered the question with lyrics from that same song: "I love you more than fame, more than wealth, more than the world." About a week or so later, I read my name in the sports page of the *Los Angeles Herald Examiner* for the last time. It was a one-line paragraph that said, "Everyone was in camp today except George Pantages." I came to the realization that day that playing football for me was not just a game, it was a god, and my God (Jesus) will not share His glory with anyone. I went from a well-known high school sports figure to an unknown college student. It ripped my heart to shreds!

My new life in Christ was nothing like I had anticipated. Believing that I had given up so much to serve the Lord, I thought I could just hit the ground running, making an impact in the Kingdom of God immediately. But there were issues that needed to be dealt with, chinks in my personality and character that needed adjusting, and that would take a great amount of time. For the first time in my life I no longer had special privileges. The slack that had been cut for me, being a well-known athlete, disappeared into thin air. I now had to wait in line like everyone else, couldn't cut classes knowing that coaches would cover for me, and I began to understand how life was lived without privileges.

Being part of an Apostolic/Pentecostal organization did me no favors as well. I had a difficult time fitting in because of my quiet nature, knowing that Pentecostals don't do "quiet" very well. There is an unwritten rule that encourages boisterous worship and expressing oneself either dancing, running the aisles, or shouting the house down. That's what Pentecost is all about NOISE and lots of it! I never felt comfortable and as much as I tried to blend in I always felt like if I was an outsider. When I had an opportunity to express myself verbally, it was always accompanied by tears. So much so that I was nicknamed "Jeremiah, the weeping prophet." My insecurities drove me away from people, but at the same time they drove me to God. I began to form a closeness with the Lord that most young people my age did not have. I figured if I could not fit in with church folk, well then maybe if I dedicated my time and efforts to minister personally unto God it would be enough to put my mind at ease.

After thirteen years of congregating in the church I was saved in, I believed I had a call to pastor my own church. Once again, the office of a pastor was nothing like I had imagined. My people skills were lacking, and I had a difficult time getting people to serve the Lord in the same manner I had been taught. I took a great leap of faith to secure a building big enough to start a daycare center that would ultimately finance all of the expenses and projects of the local church. My next error came by underestimating the time needed to stabilize our finances and manage the church in the black. When we finally ran out of money and did all that I knew to do to make things work, it ended in a bunch of broken pieces. Another heartbreak, another failure, another devastating experience that found its way into the core of my being, causing me to be wary of anything that had to deal with "faith."

As the restoration process began, I finally came to grips with my failures and decided to give it one more try. This time the Lord threw me a curve ball because He was asking me to do something and/or be someone that I thought I was completely incapable of. When the call came to evangelize, I thought He had lost His mind because I did not fit the mold of a fiery evangelist. I wasn't very "Rah-rah" in my presentation of the gospel, if you know what I mean. To add insult to injury, He was asking me to do it in a language (Spanish) that I did not have a complete command of. "Why me?" There were so many other men of God qualified and capable to do a more efficient job than me, but found out later I was the only one half-willing to accept the responsibility, so I did.

Something inexplicable happened next. Because I was willing to respond to God's call, unexpectedly the "Gifts of the Spirit" began to operate in my ministry like never before. People began to receive the baptism of the Holy Ghost by the hundreds and thousands and what was even more amazing was that a greater number of people were being miraculously healed. I'm not talking just headaches here, God was healing the blind, deaf, paralytic, cancer-stricken and more. There was so much success that in my mind it was too good to be true. You know what that meant, don't you? It was time for another HEARTBREAK! With my newfound success came a big change in our family routine. Up to that point, we as a family traveled together. But, when churches from out-of-state began to call it meant that I would have to travel alone most of the time because my children were in school. I did the best that I could keeping everything and everyone all together, but unbeknownst to me my wife began to slip spiritually. Because the enemy could not break me through hard times and losses, he decided to work on my wife. Sad to say, it worked. On the day we were to celebrate our 25th wedding anniversary, she confessed to me that she had been unfaithful. Never in my wildest imaginations would I have believed she would fall in that manner. What made it more difficult to accept was the fact that God through revelation did not show me what was going on. In the past through my ministry, God had revealed to me other infidelities that destroyed peoples' marriages. Why in the world couldn't He have done that for me? I don't know who I was angrier at, God or my wife. It was a loss that I honestly believed I would not recover from.

The breaking of the marriage vows had repercussions in that it affected not only our family, but my ministry as well. She no longer wanted to serve God in the way we had believed up to that point, so she found a less rigid way of serving Him. It was then decided to sell the one and only home we had ever owned and go our separate ways. My daughters were to stay with her, and my son

Timothy decided to stay with me. Having to pay child support placed a great burden on me financially, because when most churches found out about my divorce, they stopped inviting me to speak. I had to go out and find another source of income to help us make ends meet. Most of the times our meals consisted of two ARCO hotdogs and a drink. Occasionally, when I did have an invitation to speak and the pastor would take me out to eat after the service, I ordered an enormous amount of food (enough for two people) and took half of it home with me to give to my son. I'm sure as the pastors watched me order they were thinking, "Where in the world is he going to put all that food, he's so skinny." (Back in the day I was.) I felt if I was going to be eating good then he needed to eat good as well. He never complained nor griped, he was just happy to be eating with his dad.

Although at the time I felt I had gotten the short end of the stick with the divorce and my license to preach being revoked, I heeded the Lord's voice when He said, "Just keep your mouth shut and take it." I understood if I took that stance there was a great blessing in store for me somewhere down the road. That blessing came in the form of my future wife, Maria. When I fell in love with her, I felt as if God had taken a big eraser and erased all my heartbreak away. Although I had spent twenty-five years of my life in my first marriage, as I look back now I feel as if Maria is really the mother of my children.

Life now was too good to be true. With a woman sold out 100 percent to my ministry, her being by my side only enhanced it. A short time after I became an author, and with this book I will have written seven books in all. She typesets the books and then translates them into Spanish. I know I get all of the notoriety, but she is the one in the background pulling the strings for us to become successful. A year after being married we moved from California to Texas and things really began to blossom. We started traveling internationally to Canada, Mexico, Central and South America.

Life was truly bliss for about five years when the next heartbreak occurred, LITERALLY! In 2013, I suffered a heart attack and a stroke that disabled me for about seven months. I had been hospitalized as a child when I was recovering from polio and I pretty much knew what to expect, but this time it was worse than what I had remembered. Most of the people in my ward were there anywhere between a week to a month. I, on the other hand, left the hospital seven weeks later. It was so bad at the end they told me I had come down with hospital-itis (i.e., being sick and tired of being hospitalized).

Shortly after being checked in, I was told that the hospital had invested about $30,000 on each new bed in our ward. It had to be the most uncomfortable bed I have ever slept in in my life. It got so bad that at the end, after only ten minutes trying to fall asleep, I would transfer myself to another chair in my room. When that didn't work I would move to a lounger in my room. When that didn't work, I would use the wheelchair available to me. Finally, when that didn't work I would get on the floor. One time at bed check I was not in my bed and the nurse started to panic. When I told her not to worry because I was on the floor, she really began to freak out. I finally convinced her I was okay and had not fallen.

Of the three therapies I was required to take, speech therapy was the worst. It was there I was able to realize just how bad off I was mentally. I could not even do the easiest math problems I was required to do and my blurred vision didn't help the situation either. I knew I was really in a mess when my wife asked me one day if I could say her name. Beating around the bush, trying to find somewhere in my brain the memory of her name, I finally blurted out, "Cuqui." I was half right, you see Cuqui is her nickname. I can remember Satan mocking me, asking me if I could not even remember my wife's own name, how in the world would I ever be able to preach again? That truly was a heartbreak!

One positive byproduct of what I had to endure in the hospital was dealing with the rationing of my liquids. After a while, I had to start hiding glasses of water or juice, because if I didn't drink it at the time it was served it would be taken away. One time, mistakenly I had drunk all my water and it was time to take medication. The nurse would not allow me extra water to take it. I could not believe they were that rigid, and yet I could sense the Lord trying to teach me a lesson. "Now you know how people in hell will feel when they too are thirsting for something to drink."

Slowly but surely my resistance to the attacks from hell was breaking down. I was constantly bombarded with statements like, "You're not going to get out of here alive." I had difficulty reading because of the stroke and I felt defenseless, even more so because my memory was affected and I could not quote Scripture anymore. Like a Chinese torture drill, where they pour a drop of water on your head, little by little eventually the drop feels like a hammer busting your head wide open. That's how I felt with these attacks. Within myself I felt at times that if the enemy were to show up at that moment, I would not have the capacity to fight back. My resistance to him was very low, dwindling with each and every day. Lo and behold, on one of those days it happened.

I could sense all around me the evil presence of Satan along with his minions. I was pleading with God for help, but the closer he (Satan) got to me, the more I felt I was going to suffer a nervous breakdown. Right when I bowed my head and asked God to forgive me because I could not fight any longer and I was going to give in, the presence of the Lord appeared in my room. He slowly but surely made His way towards where I was holding my head in my hands, ready to snap. Suddenly, out of nowhere, I felt a celestial hug and felt the Lord say this. "You can't have him Satan because he belongs to me." Immediately the ugly presence left and in its place was a calming peace and I had the strength and the wherewithal to live another day for Him.

As I have continued my Christian journey through this ungodly world, each "why me?" moment has helped chisel away much of the unnecessary junk I had accumulated in my heart. It was necessary for God to be harsh at times because it was the only way it would rid me of the things that separated me from Him. I have always wondered if the apostle Paul ever found out about the conversation Ananias had with the Lord concerning this madman, Saul of Tarsus. The statement God made to Ananias that finally encouraged him to pray for Saul was eye-opening:

-- For I will show him how many things he must suffer for My name's sake. Acts 9:16

What exactly did the apostle Paul have to endure? It would be far easier to document the ways he did not suffer, because when you read his admission to his life as an apostle, it would appear that he was trying to sensationalize his life. But, in reality he concluded that the "why me?" moments were nothing more than his Lord trying to fellowship with him. When he came to that understanding it did not make the suffering any easier, but at least he understood the purpose of it all and ran with it.

At the time of this writing I have just had a second toe amputated. The sore that caused gangrene to form was not only violently aggressive, but it happened from one day to the next. For all we did to make sure an amputation would never happen again (the first one happened in 2015), it still happened. I have understood that sometimes in life you are going to lose a round or two. But, with each loss, by the grace of God we pick ourselves up again to fight another day. We don't dwell on what we have lost, because if it would have been essential God would have never let us lose it in the first place. He can still use effectively what is left over because then He is the one who receives all the credit.

WHY ME? Because if I endure, I will be more like Jesus!

Missti as a Child

Missti in the Military

The Jones Family

CHAPTER 2

Missti Jones

*****NOTE***** God will never give you more than you can bear, and just like Joseph had to be sold to save thousands of people, including his family, and learn forgiveness, so do we sometimes.

I have been a Pentecostal since I was three years old. I got the Holy Ghost speaking in other tongues when I was five and baptized in water when I was nine. My relationship with God was the only thing keeping me alive from the age of five until I got out of the Army at the age of thirty-one. This was necessary because I had to serve God all alone.

My parents were not godly people. They were drug and alcohol-addicted hippies. The age of three was the earliest I can remember, and I only know I was three at the time because my oldest brother is four years older than I am and he was starting school. I was jealous that he was learning how to read and write, and I couldn't. It was some time during that age my mother told me I had to "go play with my uncle," and I wasn't to come back until the game was over. I learned later that he wasn't my uncle, it wasn't a game he wanted to play, and by the age of nine I learned what a "prostitute" was, and that my parents were selling me to men to pay for their addictions. I had talked to my pastor when I was twelve (as far as I know he isn't a pastor anymore) and he told me that I wasn't to tell anyone because it would "give the church a bad name." I then told my public school teachers about what was going on and they called the Department of Human Services (DHS). My mother accused them of being bigots because they said I "acted different than other children" my age, and my mother said it was because I was a Christian. DHS never did anything, and I never saw the workers again. By the time I was twelve I learned why my pastor at the time didn't want to help. See, after I realized my parents were selling me to all these bad men instead of protecting me, I ran away into the woods where our dog later found me. My parents then chained me up in our chicken coop and I was given a gallon-sized pickle jar to put the money in after the men were done with me. There was an elastic hair band in the jar I was to tie the money up with and hand to my mother in the morning. At 4:30 am my mother came in with a hose and would hose me down, collect the money, and I could go to sleep, do homework, or read the one book I could have....my Bible. I was always tired in school, and I was surprised that no one in my private school even caught on to what was possibly happening to me. (Later I found out one sister in church spoke up, but no one listened to her.)

By this time my mother was coming to church, not to get God, but to monitor me so I wouldn't tell anyone anymore. I watched her on a church night take the wad of money out that had my hair band on it, and she gave a part of the wad to my pastor. When I asked what she was doing, she claimed she was paying her tithes, but I knew in the spirit it was bribe money. People, it is something to note here that ministers and people in church are HUMAN! Don't blame God, people of one sex or the other, groups, businesses, or entire churches for what one or two do! Don't let their sin become your sin! That was for free...

It was then that I had resolved in my mind to get a good education and get out of my parents' home as fast as I could. I knew marrying anyone in church was out of the question, because who would want to marry a prostitute who had been sold to men since she was three, against my will or not?! Keep in mind, this was a fourteen-year-old thinking due to being preached at in church about fornication and how dirty girls are who are not virgins, and how good godly men would never want someone like me; EVER!

Anyway, I started working moving irrigation pipe, picking berries for farmers, bucking hay (that gets rather sporty in a skirt, let me tell ya), and later became a dishwasher in an old folks home to pay my way through private Christian school. I worked really hard, and I graduated when I was seventeen. My parents had no clue when I brought them home a form to sign: they thought it was an honor roll field trip paper. In reality, it was custody papers and they signed the form without reading it, thus making me a ward of the US Army. This allowed me to enlist at the age of seventeen and escape this unbelievable nightmare.

Why the Army, some have asked? Because during the time between fourteen and seventeen years old, I prayed that God would show mercy on me and kill me. I knew I was damaged goods and not a single person on earth would care if I lived or died. I would rather die than keep being sold to men against my will. So, in my seventeen-year-old way of thinking, I thought, "I can go to Vegas and be a legal prostitute and keep all the money my parents were making off me and most likely die from some John who would kill me." My other option would be to join the Army, the only branch in the armed forces that would allow me to keep my long hair (which I gave to God when I was twelve). This also meant that I could get three meals a day, which I NEVER had before, and get to wear brand-new clothes.... even if they were uniforms they would be mine. I would have a roof over my head, and if need be I could die an honorable death. Even if God was the only one at my funeral, it would be honorable! So, I chose God and an honorable death over Satan and dying in shame as a prostitute. I told my pastor

I had enlisted and would not be in church due to being in Basic Training and AIT in Ft McClellan, Alabama.

I was then told I was not to have any contact with anyone in the United Pentecostal Church International (UPCI) from the state I was stationed in because I was not living up to the Holiness standards of the church. No writing, no phone calls, no meetings, or talking. I was on my own! I promised him I wouldn't contact anyone, and I kept my word. I eventually lived for God all alone, no church, no pastor for nearly two decades until I was medically retired from the Army. From time to time I got to attend missionary churches when I was stationed close enough to one or when I was deployed.

By this time, I was seventeen when I enlisted. I went home, and my parents were going to lock me up again and I told them if they ever sold me again, including that night, as soon as I turned eighteen and I was an adult, I would turn them over to the police, because the statute of limitations at the time for rape was nine months. I was never sold again. While I was waiting to be shipped out for basic and AIT, I asked God over and over why; why did this happen to ME?! I never heard God's voice or He giving me an answer UNTIL.......

I just got to my first duty station at Ft. Sam Houston, Texas. I was still only seventeen, just shy of turning eighteen, and was on patrol as a military police officer. I was all alone for my first time and as I was patrolling, I saw a female soldier running naked across the parking lot of the barracks where our medics go to AIT. I thought this solder was a streaker, UNTIL I saw the fear in her eyes, and on her face. I knew instantly why she was scared, because I had that same fear every time I was chained up in that chicken coop. I got out of my patrol car, ran to her with a green wool army blanket, wrapped it around her, put her in my car, and took her straight to BAMC for a rape test kit to be done on her. I asked her who raped her. She refused to talk to me, and tears just came down her eyes. I then took off my BDU coat with my rank and MP brassard on it, so I looked like a normal no rank female like her. I took both of her hands into mine and began to tell her of my story growing up and being sold to men to pay for my parent's addictions. She started bawling, and told me everything that happened, and we were able to apprehend and convict her rapist, who had raped thirteen other soldiers, both male and female, and kicked him out of the Army.

On my way home after patrol, I was listening to gospel music on the radio, as it was my "church" worship time, and I would have my Bible lesson and prayer once I got to my dorm in the barracks. Out of nowhere, while I was singing the song, God said, "This is why Missti..." It hit me so hard I had to pull over and cry, to let out years of pain and self-loathing. I thanked God that He allowed me to go through that horrible life as a kid instead of another brother or sister in the church who might have not been able to bear it and would have committed suicide instead. I thanked Him for not killing me like I had begged and got rid of that fourteen-year pity party I had been throwing for myself.

I later became the lead rape investigator on our bases, helping CID, NCIS, CIA, and MPI with cases dealing with rape and domestic violence. By sharing my testimony with the victims, I would help them get to a comfort level allowing them to eventually tell us who raped them. With this information we would be able to formally charge them and could eventually put them behind bars.

That's not all God did, though. A few years after I was in the Army, my father had to go through the Red Cross to get in touch with me. I had left my family for good and had not contacted anyone I knew from my past, just like I promised. He told me that when I left for the Army he had nightmares of Vietnam (he was an 82nd Airborne Ranger who worked Crypto in Vietnam), and all he thought about was me being captured by the North Viet Cong (NVC). At that time, he got sober and divorced my mother. No longer needing to play "church," my mother left God and married some other guy. My dad explained he had to sell the house in the divorce and was now living with a friend.

I started to cry, and God removed the hate and bitterness from me. I told my dad I forgave him, as I had just got back from Somalia where we lost eighteen men, four close friends of mine. I knew that fighting in a war was probably why he started using the drugs, and after being hooked, he just couldn't break free. I paid for my dad to get on a train to come to me. I took care of the man who once sold me to pay for his addiction until a few months before his death. God helped me to forgive him, because the forgiveness WASN'T just for him; it was also for ME. That wasn't all God did either! I had seen four doctors in two countries who all said I wouldn't be able to have children. I was okay with that because who would want to marry a woman like me? An apostolic female, who was not only sold for at least fourteen years to God knows how many men, and who was a soldier to boot?! I mean, I wasn't allowed to even go to church most of the time, and the ones I did go to, what kind of God-fearing man would even look at me, let alone think I was "wife" material after finding out my past? Today, I am a mother of five, two of whom I gave birth to, and if that is not an example of God's grace then listen to this. I am also the wife of a MINISTER! If you stay faithful to God, folks, and don't allow someone else's sin to become your sin, you can avoid hurting others both in the church and out. Your spiritual DNA will be reconfigured and let me tell you this, you are gonna like what you see.

If God can love and forgive someone like me, a woman who had not only been a prostitute (albeit against my will...that is what I was) and to love a soldier who killed several people (yes, yes it was war, but I still killed people), then THERE IS NOTHING THAT YOU HAVE DONE IN LIFE SO BAD THAT GOD WON'T FORGIVE YOU. HE WILL WRAP HIS ARMS AROUND YOU, AND WELCOME YOU BACK HOME TO HIM. I hope this testimony of mine helps you who think you are too far gone or "bad" for God to love. Give God a chance! Give yourself a chance. I will leave you with this. It was said to us as soldiers before we deployed to Afghanistan right after the 9/11 attacks, when I was stationed at Ft. Lewis, WA. I hope it encourages you, like it does me:

I AM A CHRISTIAN

Who am I?
I am a Christian!

That's right! And you need to remember that through all your battles and trials!
I will conquer what has not been conquered.
Defeat will not be in my creed.
I will believe, when others have doubted.
I will always endeavor to uphold the prestige, honor, and respect of God, and my fellow brothers and sisters in Christ.
I have trained my mind through prayer, and my body will follow.

Who am I?
I am a Christian!

I will acknowledge the fact that my enemy, the devil, does not expect me to win, nor survive.
He should know this, right now: I will NEVER surrender!
Weakness will not be in my heart!
I will look to my comrades in church, to those who have brought me into this truth, those ministers who have trained me, and I will draw strength from them!

Who am I?
I am a Christian!

*I will gladly go out into the field of spiritual battle,
And I will move, groove, and do everything I can do to defeat Satan.
I will reach my field of spiritual battle with any godly means at my disposal!
And, when I get there I will arrive violently, and take it by force!
I will rip the heart out of my enemy, the devil,
And leave it on the ground beneath me, as I worship God for the victory!
Because Satan cannot stop me!*

Who am I?
I am a Christian!

*To my sides, I have my brothers and sisters in Christ: comrades.
To my back, I have a legion of angels ready to fight alongside me.
To my front, I have the Lord Jesus Christ, who overshadows and protects me!
All have been with me through thick and thin!
Through blood, sweat, and tears!
NEVER will I let my comrades fall or fail!
NEVER will I let God, my comrades, or the angels down.
And, I will NEVER leave a brother or sister behind at the altar, in the field of battle alone!
Because our opponents, the devil and his demons, don't know my heart!*

Who am I?
I am a Christian!

No one will deny me the Word of God and His salvation!
No one will define me, as God is the author and finisher of my faith!
And, no one will tell me who and what I am, or can and cannot be, because God knew my name before I was ever born!
BELIEF will change my world!
It has moved mountains!
It has moved continents!
It has moved countries!
It has put man on the moon!
And, it will carry me through ANY spiritual battle Satan throws at me!
I will remember warriors before me, like Joshua and Caleb, and I will say in my heart, "I can take the victory!" no matter how big the trials may be!

Who am I?
I am a Christian!

"Defeat" and "Retreat"; those words are not in my vocabulary! I don't understand their definitions!
I don't always understand when things go wrong.
I don't understand my mistakes all the time.
But I do understand this: I understand God brings me the victory, and I understand never surrendering to Satan and the world!

No matter how bad things get, my heart, my mind, my faith, God's Word, and my trust in the Lord God Almighty will carry my body when my limbs are too weak.

Who am I?
I am a Christian!

Today will be that day!
Not tomorrow, and not next week!
But right now, right here!
At this altar, at this house of God, or in my home!
I will not walk, crawl, or flee from the spiritual battle I am in!
But, I will run into the field of battle with the Authority in the Name of Jesus Christ!
And, I will win this war!
History will remember me!
The demons will know my name, like they did with Jesus and Paul, and flee from me as I resist the devil!
I will not have to worry about them being kind to me, because if God be for me, then who can be against me!
God has already defined me!
I will continually sing praises to His name, and give thanks to Him, no matter what battle I am in, or mountain top I must climb to reach Him!
And no one will tell me what I can or cannot be due to my past, as God has already laid out the perfect plan for my life, and my future!
I will never go back from where God brought me!
I will not look back!

I will remember Lot's wife!
I will never quit, until I know I have given God everything my body, my mind, and my soul has to give Him, and He has called me home to be with Him!

Who am I?
I am a Christian!

NEVER FORGET WHO YOU ARE!

Arthur & Dalila Janos

The Janos Family

CHAPTER 3

Dalila Janos

He was approximately ten or eleven years old when I first saw him. I remember it clearly because he was dressed in a crisp, white dress shirt with a thin black tie, black pants and shiny black shoes. He was the most adorable child in the room. What caught my eye was the fact that he had this great big smile on his face and was holding a large Bible in his arms, cradling it like a treasure. It was in the dining hall of the Apostolic Church in Beaumont, California, where my dad was the pastor that I saw Arthur Janos for the first time. The huge smile on his face and the sparkle in his eyes showed me that he was a happy child. It piqued my interest to see who he was. Next to him was his sister, dressed in a pretty poofy dress with curly hair tied in pretty bows. Then I saw their mom; a slender young woman who was dressed beautifully with color-coordinated accessories. In her arms was another adorable baby with big squeezable round cheeks. The family was impeccably dressed and well groomed. Their mom, Martha, was escorting them to their seat so that they could eat and fellowship with everyone after the service that we had just celebrated. From that moment on, we continued to see Martha and her family off and on at different events as she attended the neighboring church of Banning. It was so adorable to see little Arthur dressed so sharp and carrying his huge Bible. He looked like a little minister in the making. Looking back, I can honestly say that it was love at first sight, yet I had no idea at that time. After all, I was six years older than him and at that time and age, I was a high school student trying to fit in.

He was around the age of fourteen or fifteen when Arthur became a member of the Beaumont church with us. We had English Sunday School classes, which Arthur's mom wanted him to attend. I remember when she spoke to my dad about him. She gave her testimony about how he was a miracle child. She said that the doctors wanted her to abort Arthur because he was supposedly deformed. She was told that he wouldn't live a long life and that his quality of life would be poor. She prayed and the Lord answered her prayer and gave her a healthy and happy baby boy with no defects whatsoever. Quite the contrary to what the doctor had predicted, he was a strong, healthy and intelligent young man. She took great care of all of her children, but Arthur was her miracle baby. She asked my father if he would allow him to congregate with us. She was very zealous over her children and wanted him to learn as much as he could and fellowship with the youth at our church. My father naturally agreed. My dad would pick up Arthur for Sunday School and he would spend the whole day with us. In those days we had Sunday School devotion, a class, and then we would return to church for more devotional time to say our memory verses and wrap up the morning Sunday School class. Then we would all eat together and wait around for the afternoon worship service. It was a special time spent together. We were a close-knit congregation and we truly enjoyed the fellowship.

Our family was always attending a lot of church events all over the place and Arthur was right there with us. My dad took him under his wing and he became like a grandson to him. In fact, when we would meet our family at the different church services, my aunts would ask us, 'Which grandson is this?' We had to explain that he was a youth from our church because they would always see him with us. As time went on, Arthur became a local youth leader and he moved up the various levels in leadership, holding several offices. He had a fine upbringing, very noble and kind, very respectful to everyone and always offering to serve others. He was quiet and reserved, but he was astute and intelligent. He was always trying to learn and better himself.

One day, as I came back from taking my mom to the grocery store, I found a cute little stuffed puppy and a glass rose in a small vase waiting for me. My brothers snickered and they said that it was from Arthur. It was so sweet because to me, it felt like it was a crush he was going through. Did I mention that he was six years younger than me? I had seen him as a brother and co-laborer. In fact, I used to get angry with him because he was the local president of our youth group and he would sometimes forget to tell me that we had the kitchen commission the next day. He would tell me, "Don't worry. I'll buy everything. You just have to cook the main dish." We normally made tacos because it was quick and easy to prepare. He later confessed that he loved working together and that he thought it was flattering how I would give in to his last-minute plans.

Well, as the years went by our friendship grew and we always had interesting and meaningful conversations. He kept asking to take me out to lunch or dinner, and I would beat around the bush with him and tell him that I would one day. That day came when I showed up at the Wells Fargo bank that he worked at on El Paseo Drive in Palm Desert, back in 1997. I had an offer that day from an attorney that I worked with and I respectfully turned him down, stating that I had other plans. I stretched the truth because I didn't want to go to lunch with him, but I actually was in the mood to have lunch with someone. As it turns out, my dear charming friend Arthur worked in the same town as I did, so I went to see if he was available. I'll never forget the look on his face when I walked in and he was walking toward the front door to go on his lunch break. It took him by surprise. We had such a nice lunch that the hour went by very fast. We ended up calling each other later that night and continued to grow our friendship even stronger. Arthur had grown into a mature, responsible and caring individual and I no longer saw him as a little boy. I saw in him a passion for God and a courteous, upstanding young man who was driven and determined. Then I remembered the little boy with the black pants and white shirt with a big old Bible in his hands. He had been groomed and mentored to be a very special young man. Anyone who knew him would agree. He was one of a kind, he was unique and personable, sociable and humorous, ready to serve instead of being served. I thank God that He opened my eyes to see what was before me, because Arthur had plans to leave for Rhode Island and pursue a career and, as he said, 'try to forget about me' because he thought that I was not interested in him.

On the day that he asked me to marry him, I thought he was going to ask me to be his girlfriend. I was blown away. When I told him that he put the cart before the horse, his response was, "Dating is to get to know a person. We've known each other for eight years. I know what God has for me. I don't need proof." He was right. I had known him for eight years and in that time, we worked together, went to services and choir practices and performances together, we served on the same youth boards. I knew where his heart was. I admired him for his patience and love and determination for staying the course and not giving up on me. It was the best decision I've ever made. He was the best husband one could ever dream of. He was always respectful. He never ever put me down or belittled me or our children. He always made time for us and always found ways to make us smile. I couldn't be mad at him because he wouldn't have it. If I went on a tangent and started to get mad, he'd take me in his arms and hold me close until I cried because he showered me with his love and tell me that nothing is worth getting so angry about. He'd then make jokes and made me laugh so hard that I couldn't possibly stay mad. He taught me so much by the way he lived his life. He continuously reminded me of God's love and mercy.

The day came when he was asked to be a pastor. The proposal was to go to a church in Texas. Our pastor told us to pray and fast for two weeks and then give our response. We did. In the beginning of my fast I was fearful and filled with doubt. I told the Lord that I was not ready and that I didn't feel like my husband was ready. He was so kind and tenderhearted, docile and too friendly. After all, I'm a PK (pastor's kid) and I knew the life we lived, being under the microscope and taking hits from every side. I knew how hard it was and I gave the Lord a list of all the reasons why I didn't think Arthur was ready. Thinking back to that time, I know I wanted to protect him. When I presented my mental list of the reasons why I felt Arthur was not ready, God's response to me was, 'I don't give lists, nor do I pay attention to them with you; why would I do that with him?' So then my response was, "Why Texas? I don't think I can go to Texas!" And His response to me was, "Where could you go that I wouldn't be with you?" That was enough for me to throw up my banner of surrender and follow my husband, to let the Lord do what He was going to do in our ministry together. Arthur didn't know about the list that I was going to bring to him. I couldn't bring myself to tell him. Chapter 13 of Corinthians kept repeating in my mind, and when the Lord spoke to me in the manner that He did, He confirmed what I was feeling in my spirit. I couldn't get in the way of what God was about to do. Arthur was already determined and knew what plan of action he would take. He was just waiting on me.

We prepared ourselves to meet with Bishop President Daniel Sanchez. On the road to the General Office Headquarters, Arthur asked me to quiz him on the Constitutional By-Laws. He was nervous and praying that he would 'pass the test.' We met for two hours with Bishop Sanchez. The very first thing he said to us was that we were not there to be approved because we were already approved. He told us that we were there to receive counsel. Toward the end of this sincere, amazing counseling session, Bishop Sanchez told us that there was another church that he wanted us to consider. He gave us the option to choose between Texas or Oregon. He told us to pray about it and even visit each place so that we could make our decision. We were to give our decision in two weeks. We were overjoyed and amazed. Immediately Arthur stated, "Who gets a second choice?" He had decided not to visit any of the two churches. He didn't want his mind to be swayed by appearances or pretenses. He sought the direction of God, fully relying on His guidance. Well, in the two weeks that we were given, Arthur took on the process of applying for work in both states near both towns. He started looking for homes to live in and we prayed for God's direction. Both towns had promising jobs with each of them calling him for further interviews. The job in Salem, Oregon, told him that he came in second and that they gave the job to the other applicant. They told him that they were going to keep his resume on file. Again Arthur submitted resumes and made phone calls to everything from moving vans to rental agencies and beyond. The end of the two weeks was near and nothing had come to fruition. As he was telling one of his best friends about what was happening, he was asked, "What are you going to do if you don't find anything?" His response was, "I'm still going regardless of this situation. That's not going to stop me." Nobody was returning his calls and he was getting anxious; so much was his anxiety that he couldn't sleep one night. I felt him tossing and turning and he finally got up and went into the living room. He came back and slept like a baby. That very next morning he received a call from the bank in Salem, offering him a job because the first applicant turned it down. The home rental agency called him and told him that we were approved for a home and the moving company called, giving him the best rate that we could afford. He was amazed. He told me how he had been stressing about it and prayed the most fervent prayer he had ever prayed in his life and felt like a load had been lifted when he asked the Lord to take over because he was done trying. Sure enough, the doors had opened up and everything fell into place for us to go to Oregon. I believe it's important to note that Arthur was reading a book called *The Barbarian Way*, by Erwin McManus, that truly made an impact on him. He credited that book with helping him to step out in faith. He loved to read and had a great collection of over 400 books.

The day that we arrived in Woodburn, Oregon, to celebrate the ceremonial installation service, our son Benjamin was five and our daughter Emily was nine. Benjamin was so excited that he could hardly wait for the car to stop before he ran out of it to get to meet everyone. Benjamin has the same excitement and determination as his papa. He was eager to meet new people and make new friendships. Emily was calm and a little more cautious, but she too was eager to start this new life with her family. Everyone was so friendly and loving. Our reception was heartwarming and sincere. We quickly got to know everyone and we dove right in. I learned that everything goes smoothly when you're connected with God. He opened our eyes and guided us along the way. We had our struggles, but God prevailed at all times. There was a time when we were seeking for a church of our own, and a building that the congregation had sought out before we arrived came up for rent. The members explained to my husband that they had previously declared this building as their future building by walking around it seven times. The building was run down and needed a lot of repairs. When another church rented it out, our congregation found it hard to believe that the building was not meant for us. It was about a year later that my husband saw it for rent again. The church prayed about it and the Lord opened the doors for this building to be rented by us with the option to be purchased. Turns out that the previous renters had made all the necessary remodeling and repairs, only to end up having to leave. It was first priced at a high rent that we weren't able to afford, but the owner took a liking to my husband, or as my mom would say, 'God granted grace' in the eyes of the owner toward my husband so that a deal was made and thus a friendship was formed between the two men.

We were there six years and on the verge of entering into a new lifestyle in the summer of 2015. At that time my husband was going to quit his full-time job of managing two branches of the bank and was to dedicate himself to become a full-time pastor. He was deeply involved in the community as the president of the chamber of commerce, a member of the local hospital board, a board member of the nearby Literacy Center, as well as the secretary of the district general ministerial board, aside from being a pastor. He wanted to establish a presence in the community in an effort to bring them together in different collaborations. His influence in the community was felt far and wide. As part of his collaborations, he would speak at one of the nearby colleges, giving presentations on servant leadership. He believed that servant leadership was living by example to offer to serve instead of being served. He made a lasting impression in his community. He worked fervently to do his best at every position he had. On the day of his passing (he died of a heart attack), he gave a short "lesson" / presentation to the board members of the chamber of commerce. He talked about setting goals and used an analogy about a boat. His notes were entitled, "Are you a paddler, passenger, or an anchor?" He left an impact on one member who talked to us about how his message made him reflect on the life of the apostles. He was supposed to meet Arthur for dinner that night and was excited to talk to him about the lesson further.

Upon hearing of his untimely death, I cannot even put into words how I felt. I never had the opportunity to say goodbye and my life from one moment to the next was in complete chaos. On the day of his funeral, numerous people from the community showed up to pay their respects and found a joyful service that celebrated Jesus the way Arthur would celebrate Jesus. Arthur loved to worship God. He always wanted songs that had true meaning to worship God. He would sit and meditate for hours listening to worship music as he drew inspiration from the Holy Spirit. It was such a beautiful thing to see and listen to.

He finished his race. The legacy that he left behind in the way that he lived his life will never be forgotten because it proved that he was a God-fearing man who loved the Lord and was filled with His Spirit, which was clearly demonstrated. That impact and legacy are seeds that were planted in the lives of many, many people. Those seeds are many and they were spread throughout a wide range of diverse cultures and backgrounds where God Himself deemed necessary. As I sit here and write, I'm reminded of the different organizations that he was a part of and the people that we met along the way, whom he impacted. That's a life well lived, a life that was not wasted, but a life poured out to the very last drop, which glorified God and reflected His love and mercy. Many of these people came up to me and told me how he impacted their lives. One of his coworkers said that she was timid and afraid to talk to her boss (Arthur) because previous managers had made her feel inept. She said that even when she knew she made a mistake, Arthur never pointed it out or made fun of her. He explained the way things should go and gave her encouragement. Another employee told me that he was ready to give up on finding a better job for himself because he didn't have his G.E.D. Arthur connected him with one of the local literacy programs that he was involved in and this young man received his G.E.D. Arthur went on to hire him at the bank that he managed and this young man came to me in tears, stating how thankful he was that Arthur took an interest in him and gave him a second chance. He prayed with them and helped them focus on Christ as the answer to their lives.

Since my husband passed away a year ago at the time of this writing, I've been struggling to cope with it all. On the surface I'm strong and victorious, but hidden in the shadows I'm frail, torn, beaten down (2 Corinthians 4), etc., etc., etc. When I keep myself busy and focused on anything else but him, I'm doing great. But when my focus is on him and how much I miss him and need him and want him, I turn to mush without a backbone or purpose in life. I literally tune out everyone and dwell on the whole circumstances that I find myself in. Of course, the obvious question that I shouldn't ask, but inevitably do ask, is "Why?" And right behind it follows "How?" How could this be? I work out every scenario and probability in my mind and always come to the same conclusion. It's done. No matter what I ask or demand a response to, it is finished.

The life we shared was not in vain and was lived to the fullest as we knew it. I can honestly say that his life impacted millions. I can say that with blessed assurance, because the way he lived his life was contagious. He had a way of bringing out the best in others. He definitely did that with me and his children. We benefited the most! The way you impact millions is you set the example and you set the bar high and you surpass it. When you impact one life, that life is then shared with everyone in that person's life and so on and so forth. At his funeral he had well over 500 members of the church, district, banking and business community present. His funeral was beautiful and in my eyes just what put the icing on the cake. We celebrated Jesus and His resurrection and His coming for all those who have the hope of glory in their lives like Arthur did. His whole life's purpose and joy for living was revealed to those he impacted. I was amazed! The amount of people who showed up, besides the local church was a great contingent from the Oregon district. This reflected the lives he touched both far and wide. In support they came and in rejoicing they left because they got to see what filled this man's heart. He led by example, and to some it was unconventional. He lived his life in the trenches and dealt with the everyday person. He was always dressed immaculately so that nothing about him, including his appearance, was offensive. People respected that and it was admirable. He never wasted a moment, although his patience was continuously tried in many circumstances. He recognized the opportunity to turn it around for good.

The disciples are recorded as doing the work of baptizing, and John 1:33 states that Jesus is the one who baptized with the Holy Spirit. His job has never stopped. What I want to say by that statement is to reveal what was revealed to me. The more I look at the life of my husband, the more I see the life of Christ in him and his modeled life and example of living like Jesus did. He gave leadership conferences at a local university every year entitled, "The Servant Leader." He expressed the vision that being a leader meant being a servant. He had a way of touching the hearts of many through the way he lived his life. Even as Christ had his skeptics my husband had them too. But to those who got to walk with him, they truly got to see the heart and passion for Christ. No wonder my heart grieves so much. Without him I was feeling without purpose and less than worthy to continue in ministry. I fell into a deep pit and longed for comfort and a break from fighting the good fight because it was wearing me thin spiritually.

I longed for a friend to console me and to reach out because the voices in my head were telling me so. "Where are the friends who you've been there for?" "Where are the words of consolation that you should be getting at this time?" "Why haven't you reaped what you have sown yet? "Why hasn't God caused someone to think of me, to show me that He loves me?" I was having a pity party. I was feeling sorry that I had lost such a great love, but was not thankful for the privilege and honor to have shared his life. Nonetheless, I wanted a friend like Proverbs 17:17. But despite the accusations and doubts that were clouding my head, Christ spoke and brought to remembrance all the words of comfort that I had given and reminded me that He put them there in the first place and that that's truly all I needed. He's that Proverbs 17 friend. So I recited them in my head over and over and I started to speak them over my life and then it happened. It was as if He called my name and I resurrected once again. The spoken word is so powerful! I realized that He allowed that death, just like He allowed Lazarus' death, for His honor and His glory. A study on 2 Corinthians 4 epitomizes why Christ does what He does, even when physical death comes to your home. The end result is His glory and it's all worth it. The weight of this life is nothing compared to the weight of glory in eternity. Our life is but a tiny speck compared to eternity.

So, I rose and before I rose I knelt and I thanked Him and He loved me and showed me what my purpose was and always has been and how important it was to continue in it. It's so simple, it seems ridiculous. We expect sometimes that we're supposed to reach the masses the conventional ways that other people expect. God wants us to use the gifts we have to the fullest. Whatever you do, do it unto the Lord. Do it with all your heart and give it all, leaving nothing undone. He showed me that I am and always have been a writer. The thoughts and ideas He's put in my head over the course of my life are my purpose and destiny. They are the plans He has for me (Jeremiah 29:11-13). He showed me how important it is to let someone know you care. He wants us to speak it. He wants us to let our light shine. He wants us to seize the moment. When He brings someone to your mind, instantly pray for them and go beyond that and let them know that you are praying for them. When you're actually and physically talking to them and know there's a need, don't just say you're going to pray for them; stop what you're doing and pray together with them. Ask His Spirit to come over them and fill them with His peace that surpasses all understanding. They came into your life because they have come for a purpose. Your purpose is Christ. He wants to reveal Himself in their lives. You plant the seed, He'll bring the increase.

After these revelations and new life comes again, it's good to be alive. Everything has new meaning again and is appreciated all the more. I understand more clearly the term Paul used when he said, "I die daily" for the sake of the cross and the furthering of the gospel. Whatever may come my way, let it be to the honor and glory of Christ. Let our lives be a reflection of Him who gave His all for us so that we could embrace a glorious eternity.

Jennifer Brown

Jennifer & Mom

CHAPTER 4

Jennifer Brown

Life is unpredictable. When we are born we come into this world with our hearts wide open and full of love. We depend on the parents God gave us to protect us, love us, nurture us and provide for us. Unfortunately, for many life may or may not work out that way. I was born to a sixteen-year-old girl who was determined to keep me and raise me. My father was never active in my life, leaving when I was two. My mom was single most of my life, she worked and did the absolute best she knew to do. My mom became a Christian and received the Holy Ghost when I was three years old, speaking in tongues for the first time.

I was a scrawny, blue-eyed blonde-haired little girl with a lot of fear and anxiety. These negative traits followed me into my teenage years, and I remember on many occasions while driving up to our apartment getting physically sick due to fear. I would beg to go to my grandparents' house. There was a peace and security there for me. I mean, come on, everything is always better at grandma's house.

Let's fast forward a few years. I loved church camp. I went from eight years old until I was a teenager. I met many wonderful friends at camp, many I still have today. You would think at church camp you would never experience the pain of being teased or bullied. I truly believed that church camp would be a safe place where hurtful wounds would never be inflicted on me. Oh, but it happens, more than you'll ever know. Church camp is where I experienced wounds that would cause my heart to close. I have had many situations and circumstances in my life where I allowed my heart to close further. My trust had been broken and I had felt abandonment in a way that I never thought was possible. Loneliness was my constant companion and my self-confidence was obliterated.

Instead of turning to a loving God who was waiting for me and ready to take it all away, I instead chose to keep it in, harboring grudges and building walls of isolation. I allowed my circumstances to make me an angry, bitter and resentful person. Don't forget I was going to church, sitting on a pew, hearing the word of God and doing my Sunday impersonation of a godly young lady, yet just going through the motions. I had heard many powerful sermons in my life and I had felt the touch of the master's hand many times. But, I still chose to wake up day after day, vowing to keep my anger, bitterness and resentment intact. I kept my heart guarded, trusting no one, not even the God who created me. I made clear-cut vows to let no one in past a certain point, whether family or friend, it made no difference. There was a big sign on my heart that read, "**THIS IS AS FAR AS YOU ARE ALLOWED.**" I had securely built my ten-foot walls and added the barbed wire fence for extra security, making sure no one got in. The problem though was that nothing could get out either. I lived a lonely life really.

Oh I had many friends, but they were just kept at a distance for my protection. At the time I really did not know how to love. I had allowed my past circumstances and situations to taint my ability to love. Not only did it handicap my ability to give love, but also to receive love. Open up my heart? Ha, no way, not gonna happen. Don't forget I was still sitting on a pew, hearing sermons and going through the motions, yet I honestly loved my miserable, angry, resentful and lonely life. But not for the reasons you think. I loved it because it was familiar, comforting, and took no effort. Let's just be real, I honestly was not living life at all. I mean, I went on vacations, went to conferences, met up with friends for fun nights out. Truly living? Nope, not at all. I chose to spend a lot of time hiding behind, or should I say getting lost in, my TV shows, movies, etc. I was consumed by them and it was what I lived for. This allowed me to escape reality and enter into a fantasy world where I did not have to think or deal with my own harsh reality. I was hooked, or better yet, addicted, I had to watch the latest

TV shows, see the latest movies, and buy the newest gossip magazines.

These things were my comfort, my go-to, my security, but all these things only fed my flesh, making it more difficult to form the personal relationship God wanted to have with me. I never once chose to care for or feed my spiritual man. When you neglect the spiritual man and you allow your flesh to rule day after day, it's hard to relinquish or surrender all of the garbage harbored in your heart. You are convinced you are okay and you become comfortable with your sidekicks, anger, bitterness and resentment. They become your family, telling you that you are just fine like you are and you need no one else. Ultimately convincing you that you can't live without them. I had adjusted and adapted my life to make room for them. I was convinced this was my life and no changing needed. Let me just say, it is the enemy's good pleasure to keep us bound by what he convinces us to believe and what we accept and live with in our hearts and minds daily. Your life is a reflection of what you are allowing to grow in your life's garden.

The Bible teaches us "we reap what we sow." What harvest are you allowing to dominate in your life's garden? At this particular time I had chosen to allow anger, bitterness and resentment to overtake my garden. I had welcomed them, made them comfortable and gave them the attention they needed to dominate and grow easily. I did not realize it at the time, but God had a plan that was about to turn my world both upside down and inside out.

On January 8, 2017, it was just an ordinary Sunday of going to church, leading kid's church and going through the motions. I had no idea God had orchestrated a life-changing event for me that day. I currently lived with my stepdad, Mom, niece and nephew. I had been resting in the recliner, watching a TV show on my iPhone. My mom was asleep on the couch, and I was not sure what the others were doing. I was starving, so I got up to go get something to eat. I remember getting the food out of the refrigerator and looking at my mom and asking her if she was asleep. The next thing I knew, I was waking up in the cath lab at the hospital, asking, "Where am I?" "What happened?"

Here is what I was told happened. My mom was asleep on the couch and suddenly she heard the loudest noise, so loud it woke her up and the others came running. She said all she could see were my feet at that point and I was not moving. When she got to me I had literally dropped dead on the kitchen floor, which was tile, by the way. Immediately my mom started doing CPR. She began to pray frantically in Jesus' name as she did chest compressions. As my mom was doing CPR, she finally got a pulse but it was short-lived and my heart stopped again. My stepdad was calling 911 and praying also.

Once the paramedics reached our home, they took over and had to shock my heart to get a pulse. Meanwhile my mom, in total hysteria, was calling on the church to pray. Back to waking up in the hospital, I was informed I had a massive heart attack and would need to undergo triple bypass surgery. Heart attack? I was only forty-one years old! They had already completed a heart cath, which let them know I had three severely blocked arteries.

When I woke up in the cath lab they were in the process of doing a CT scan to check for any head trauma or brain damage. Kinda important, since I did hit the tile floor. I am thankful to report no brain damage or head trauma was found. That's the awesome God we serve. The outcome could have been a lot different. Being the stubborn person I was, when I was told I needed surgery, I boldly stated nope, no surgery for me. My current scenario was that I had a pump inserted into my leg, literally pumping the blood to my heart through my body to stay alive. I could not move my leg and it was day two of lying flat on my back, the only way I could be. I for sure needed the surgery.

After putting the doctor off for a few days, I received a stern but encouraging talk from my mom and I grudgingly consented. I had no clue what I was in for. I have to share this first of many miracles in my testimony. When the surgeon began talking to my family about the surgery (triple bypass), he was unsure if he would be able to do the bypass and stents were for sure out due to my arteries being so small. My mom asked no questions, she understood fully what that meant. She instead turned to our prayer leader from church and my church went on a twenty-four-hour around the clock prayer chain for me before and during surgery. The word of God says in Matt 21:22, "Whatever things you ask in prayer believing, you will receive."

On the day of surgery, it was early in the morning and I remember my mom saying they were there to take me for surgery. Big tears filled my eyes. I was not at a place in my life at that time to realize my life was at a crossroad, it was decision-making time and God loved me enough to orchestrate this journey and what I was about to encounter. I know I had many people covering me in prayer while I was in surgery, for which I'm forever thankful.

Back to the miracle, I know you were wondering. Once the surgery was complete, the doctor came and informed my family and all the many friends that had been there for hours on the progress. His first words were, "I was able to fix all three arteries," a direct result of the many prayers that had gone up to our Creator on my behalf. Two days later I was brought out of sedation. Of course, no one filled me in on what I would wake up to. Chest tube, IV's and literal wires in my body. My chest had been cracked open and I awoke to the dreaded breathing tube/ventilator. Three hours later, after a grueling process, I was finally able to get the breathing tube/ventilator out. I was able to breathe on my own with no oxygen needed. I was in the hospital ten days with IV's, tubes and wires all over, but hey, I was alive. This was literally just the beginning of my recovery and my journey.

I was discharged from the hospital ten days after being admitted. I was released with what is called a "life vest," but I called it a "torture vest." The reason I was released with the vest was that my infraction rate was low and doctors were trying to make sure I did not have a repeat of the previous episode. The function of the vest was to shock my heart, and if need be actually restart my heart, in case of any unforeseen circumstances. Thank you, Jesus, I never needed it. When I was discharged from the hospital, I was told I would have to wear the vest for about two months while my heart was healing. I went home wearing the vest to a hospital bed in the living room, temporarily. I had to adjust to a whole new way of life. I had to eat differently, and take medication, I had to have help in every capacity of my life. The independent girl that had built my walls and fences to keep people out all of the sudden needed people. I needed help to do everything, and I hated it. My walls and my fences were securely intact, guarding my heart like Fort Knox. My chest had been cracked open. It was numb and swollen and stayed that way for about five months. I was left with a scar that has faded but will never go away. Needless to say, I was a mess and convinced my life would never be what it once was. Which in hindsight is funny, because my life has not yet returned to what it once was.

  Let's fast forward to March. It had been about two months since my heart attack and I still had the torturous life vest. By this time I had moved back upstairs to my room and was able to sleep in my beloved bed. Things had returned to semi normal, I was not released to go back to work just yet, so I was filling my day with cardio therapy three times a week and of course my fav TV shows, movies, etc. I had grown weary in wearing the life vest, my nights were sleepless and filled with severe anxiety. I literally thought I was losing it. The sleeplessness and anxiety lasted for months, and then adding in the sudden outburst of tears, it was awful. By now three months had passed. I was SOOO ready to get the life vest off. They did an echo, which showed my infraction rate had not gone up enough. I was so disappointed, this not only meant the life vest stayed on, but possibly I would have to have a defibrillator implanted. I went home totally defeated and depressed.

My mom called me from prayer meeting that night, saying God had spoken to her and that if I would activate my faith He would heal me completely. So I made up my mind to activate my faith the best I knew how. It was now April and I still had the life vest. April was the beginning of change for me. I attended a SHINE ladies conference in Katy, TX. The speaker that night spoke about holiness and guarding the treasure of your heart. I sat there listening intently, but something was different. The message had spoken to me and resonated with me, prompting a change in me. I will never forget it. As I prayed with my friend from church, it felt like what I was praying with her for, I was praying over my own self. Crazy, I know, but that was really what happened. I finished praying with my friend and I began to weep. God touched me deeply and that was the beginning of the demolition of the fence and walls I had securely built around my heart.

I'm not sure if you believe in divine intervention or God bringing people in your life at just the right time. He surely does though, without a doubt. You see, I still had my anger, bitterness and resentment, my walls were coming down, but I still had them. God knew I needed a godly mentor, someone who knew how to get past the fence and the walls I had built, with His help of course. Remember, I trusted no one, but for some reason I allowed myself to trust this person. I began to open up and more and more my fences came down and my walls began to crumble. The more I let go and opened up and trusted my mentor, I realized I was also learning to open up and trust the most important person of all, my Creator.

As I began to feed my spiritual man and activate my faith, I realized I no longer had a desire for the things I used to fill my days with. My passion and my desire for a relationship with my Creator now consumes me. My delight is in Him. One month had passed by and it was time once again to see if the life vest could be removed. I began to ask the echo tech what she saw as she was doing the echo. She explained to me that when someone had a severe heart attack, as I did, one of two things happen. The part of the heart that dies during the heart attack stays that way or it could spark back to life. We finished the echo and I went to another room to await the results. I started crying, I so wanted it to be a good report and get that life vest off. The doctor came in and said, "I have good news." She stated the infraction rate was not where they wanted it to be, but was high enough to take off the vest. I burst into tears and then I began to thank my God for yet another miracle. You see, not only did I get to ditch the torturous life vest for good, it also meant no defibrillator implant surgery. The doctor explained some people, because of fear, still get a defibrillator implanted and I could do that if I wanted. I was like, no way. I told her it was a miracle and the God that brought me this far was not gonna fail me now.

The lesson I learned in wearing the life vest was to trust God and His timing. He was waiting on me to give Him my faith and trust completely. I have learned in making my Heavenly Father a priority, by spending time with Him, praying, and reading His word that He is never too busy. He actually loves and adores me. The more I seek Him, the more I find Him. The closer I get to Him, my old friends anger, bitterness and resentment no longer rule my life's garden. I have allowed my Creator to uproot my garden planting joy, peace, love and true happiness. God spoke this scripture to my heart: Ezekiel 36:26, "I will give you a new heart and put a new spirit within you; I will take the heart of stone out of your flesh and give you a heart of flesh." I began to weep as God spoke to me, saying "Not only did I change your physical heart but your spiritual heart as well."

Through my journey I have learned to trust my Creator. My relationship with Him is the most important one in my life. I have learned as I draw closer to Him my love is unreserved and without walls. In my relationship with Him, He has taught me to trust again. In my relationship with Him, I have learned to see myself as He sees me: beautiful, fearfully and wonderfully made in His image. In my relationship with Him I am fulfilled. In my relationship with Him I've learned it's okay to not have the walls and fences in place for protection. You see, my Creator has got me. When I do face adversity or offenses come and trust is broken again, instead of allowing those things to take root and grow in my garden, I have learned to take it to the feet of the Master and leave it. Because I have spent time with Him, and I have built a relationship with Him, I am confident, and I know He will never hurt me, break my trust, or abandon me. I am secure in my relationship with my Heavenly Father. I have by no means mastered all the above. This walk is daily. I have to make the choice daily to love, trust, and forgive if need be. I am thankful that God loved me enough to look past the walls, anger, bitterness and resentment. To see who He created with divine purpose, destiny and anointing. I choose today to walk into and step into all God has for me, no turning back.

    My heart is anchored to my Creator and I will never be satisfied with anything less. I would walk this journey again if need be to have the peace and fulfillment and relationship with my Heavenly Father. I thank you, Jesus, for every wound, for all the broken trust and heartbreak. Without all of those things, I would not be the beautifully broken but mended vessel you created me to be.

Tyler Jesse & John Moore

The Moore Boys

The Moore Family

CHAPTER 5

John Moore

A bruised reed shall he not break, and the smoking flax shall he not quench… Isaiah 42:3 (KJV)

The first time I held him, just moments after he was born, I knew my life had changed forever. There are no words to describe how you feel in the moment you realize you've become a parent. It happens instantaneously, the second you hold that child in your arms, knowing they can do nothing for themselves, they are totally dependent upon your actions. It is at that moment one of life's great questions is answered: would I willingly give my life to save someone I love? Immediately it changes from being a question to an emphatic statement: I would willingly give my life to save this child. Even though I was not living for God at that time in life, I knew enough to ask Him to help me be a good father. Unlike my own father, I vowed to God I would never leave my son with the lingering questions of love that an absent father had left with me. With all the faith I could muster at that moment, I told God I needed Him to make me a good father, a better father than I had known. Only later would I realize that God was using this moment, as He would other moments, to draw me closer to Him; just as James 4:8 (KJV) states, *"Draw nigh to God, and he will draw nigh to you."*

Tyler Jesse Moore came into this world at 7:05 PM Central Standard Time on March 14, 1996. I sat in a rocking chair inside a darkened hospital nursery, holding and staring at this beautiful child I was so proud to call my son. In that moment, my mind filled with dreams about who and what he would become; never could I have imagined nor would I have believed anyone had they told me that in sixteen short years he would be gone. However, at that moment nothing but the beauty of that child and my love for him. His life would have an immediate impact on me, yet I also knew that the current circumstances would have a longer term effect on him. His mother and I had separated shortly before his birth. Divorce was inevitable, and as a child of divorce I knew firsthand the questions and doubts he might have concerning his father. As I asked God to help me be a good father, I also promised that I would do everything in my power to take an active role in his life and never leave him wondering if he was loved by his father. To this day, I truly believe the heartfelt dialogue I had with God that night was the beginning of Him drawing me closer to Himself.

The next few years seemed relatively uneventful. He and his mother lived in San Antonio while I lived in Dallas, a difference of roughly 275 miles. Every other weekend I would drive four hours one way to visit him. No matter my financial circumstances, God always made a way for me to see him. I believe God was honoring my commitment and ensuring I was able to keep it, thus I began to desire more of a relationship with God. While my own father had not given me anything to speak of, he did introduce me to the Creator of all things. I felt it my duty to my son also to introduce to Jesus Christ. First things first, I had to fix my relationship with God before I could be an example to him. As the years went by, my relationship with TJ flourished well, considering the circumstances. Even more, my relationship with God greatly flourished, and in 2001 I married a woman God used to bring me completely into His fold. By the time TJ was five years old, we were regularly attending and greatly involved in church. He would go to church with us during visits on Sunday mornings, and the staff and the children made him feel loved and welcome. TJ was very introverted, yet these outgoing people of God made an impact that would stay with him for the rest of his life. From 2001 – 2007, TJ was able to see his father transformed by God, yet he also was able to learn about the love of Jesus and experience it firsthand. He was able to attend several children's revivals at our church, along with several Vacation Bible School events. One event stands out as a great moment for TJ; during one of the children's revival services with Reverend Lloyd Squires, there was a contest for wearing the most odd clothing combination. TJ was very excited to participate, so my wife and I helped him put together his outfit for the evening. He wore two different socks, two different shoes, a wild designed t-shirt, and bright pink pajama pants with polka dots. I recommended the pants, but since they were my wife's, TJ was hesitant at first since they were "girl pants," yet we convinced him it tied the ensemble together. At the end of the evening, he was announced as the winner. As the children cheered wildly, he walked across the stage to receive his prize; tears filled my eyes as I watched him timidly walk up to Rev. Squires. The look on his face was priceless. He would tell me later that he had no idea so many kids liked him. As an introvert, TJ was often on the outside looking in. He would have few friends in his lifetime, but he would prove to be a loyal and true friend. This moment of celebration would be the key God used to open his heart and become comfortable, and even look forward to attending church.

In 2007, I was transferred to Fredericksburg, Texas. Within a year of arriving, the church honored me by electing me as assistant pastor. Shortly after we arrived in Fredericksburg TJ's mother was deployed to Iraq. This meant he would be coming to live with us. While not exactly an ideal way for this to occur, it was a huge prayer answered. For many years I had prayed for an opportunity to have my son stay with me for a lengthy time. I firmly believed this would allow us to move into a deeper bond and relationship with each other, but also help him learn more about the God that we faithfully served. He arrived to us in early November 2008. He was twelve years old when he arrived and would turn thirteen before going back to San Antonio; God had placed him with me at a crucial time in his growth and development. I could sense his timidity upon arriving; aside from his regular visits, TJ had never known life away from the daily living with his mother and grandparents. In addition to the new environment, he was well aware that his mother would be in a combat zone somewhere in Iraq. My wife and I prayed for God's guidance in this situation, as it was apparent to us how fragile the situation would be. The first few weeks were uneventful, there were some adjustments, but nothing major developed. My wife was eight months pregnant when TJ arrived. We already had a six-year-old son, Jacob, who loved TJ. In fact, when TJ would come to visit, everyone and everything took a distant second place to his big brother. Within a few weeks of TJ moving in, we welcomed Daniel. He was born under duress and would spend several weeks in the NICU (Neo Natal Intensive Care Unit) with Meconium aspiration. After the first week, he was flown to Austin to a better facility, but after two weeks, we were able to bring Daniel home in what was a miraculous turn around. My mother had known a family who had lost a baby for the same issue just two weeks before Daniel was born. To say that we were facing a lot of stress in a short period of time seems like an understatement. Yet during this time, TJ was able to witness us in prayer, and see our church family in Fredericksburg rally around us, something he had never witnessed. Again, God was using this to open his eyes to His wondrous works and the purpose of the body of Christ. The church in Fredericksburg was considerably smaller and was only a year old when we began to attend. As the assistant pastor, I was well engaged in helping with the various aspects of the church. Pastor Don Steadman and his wife, Sharon, eagerly welcomed TJ when he arrived. I had to explain to them that TJ was an introvert and over time they would see a subtle difference in his behavior to validate his love for them. They would come to love TJ and he them. He would also come to love the members of Calvary Pentecostal Church. In January 2009, I was officially notified that my unit would deploy to Iraq later in the year. My departure would coincide with his mother returning from Iraq. My wife and I had been talking about starting a weekly family prayer night, so at this time it seemed ideal to begin. We did a lot of research looking for some pre-made plan or canned lesson we could follow. I could not believe there was nothing like that available. As necessity is the mother of invention, we made up our own plan. Monday nights would be sacred family night; no activities would be intentionally scheduled on Monday for this reason. We also decided we should pray out loud to show the boys how to pray. My wife had learned while teaching Sunday school about the JOY method of prayer for kids. It works like this:

Jesus first,
Others' needs second
Your needs last

We bought a weekly family devotional book, but also allowed the boys to pick praise songs to sing. We would open up with praise songs, then read the devotion. After the reading, we would let the boys discuss the lesson, then we would move into prayer. We would all kneel around the couch. I would begin with praise and thanks to the Lord, and when I was finished I would tap my wife and she would do the same, with the boys following this pattern as well. At first they would just repeat what Lorena and I would say as we prayed, but within three weeks they began to praise God for their own blessings. Calling out things that surprised us, even more they began to pray for others, like teachers or friends; even other people in the church who had asked for prayer. Almost weekly I would cry silently as I listened to these young hearts seeking God in sincere petition. Between February and April I was traveling frequently in preparation for deployment. In fact, I was gone for six weeks with two one-week breaks back home during that period. I was worried the praying we had started would falter in my absence. I called my wife that first Monday I was gone and asked if they had prayed. She told me that she wasn't going to push it since I wasn't there, but when the time came for prayer, TJ asked her if they were going to pray. When she asked the boys if they wanted to pray, they both responded with a resounding yes. I could hear the emotion in her voice, as she fought the tears. I too was so proud, but more thankful that God had become real to my children.

During my absence, TJ took up the mantle of helping Lorena with some of the chores and with baby Daniel. He also began to do his schoolwork, something that had been problematic before he arrived. It was obvious God was working in his life. In April, the church had a ground breaking ceremony on land purchased for a building. At that time, we rented space in an office park. TJ was very excited to participate and witness this church growth. Because of my travels, we had delayed getting Daniel dedicated. My sister Nancy came to visit for the event. As we were preparing Daniel, TJ approached her and asked her what it meant to be dedicated. She explained the process to him, he thought about it for a few minutes, then told her that he wanted to be dedicated also. Nancy came to me with tears in her eyes, for she had been praying that someday TJ would come to know God. She asked me if I thought we could bring TJ up as well to be dedicated. Pastor Steadman enthusiastically said yes, and he presided over the dedication of both boys. Jacob had been dedicated in Austin years before, yet TJ was not present for that event.

As summer approached, I asked him if he would be interested in going to Youth Camp. There was some hesitation on his part, but he decided to go. I called Seth Simmons in Austin, as he was coordinating the event. I had known Seth and his wife Sarah from our time at New Life in Austin. Seth had been the youth minister there for a number of years and was now working as a section youth leader; I trusted that he and Sarah would look out for TJ. When he returned from camp, we could all sense a change in him. He seemed more outgoing than before. Seth reported to me that TJ had gone to the altar and had been moved by God in a mighty way. He stated he did not hear him, but saw stammering lips as he sought the spirit of God. As I stated before, TJ was an introvert. His worship in church up until that time consisted of some hesitant hand clapping and some whispering soft singing. When he returned from camp, he clapped more enthusiastically and sang with the rest of the congregation. You could see the joy of the Lord emanate from his face, he was forever changed. In August, it was close to the time for him to return to San Antonio. During service one Sunday evening, Pastor Steadman was preaching about water baptism in Jesus' name. TJ asked me if he could be baptized. The pastor said yes, however we were still in the office park so if we were going to baptize him, we would have to go find a water source. Pastor Steadman asked me if I wanted to baptize my son. I accepted with a huge grin. We wound up at Lady Bird Johnson State Park where a small creek flowed. TJ and I walked a ways out into the water, and I asked him to explain to me the purpose of baptism. He told me that it was a step of faith and for the remission of sins as stated in Acts 2:38 and obedience to God's word. As I baptized my son, my heart was filled with so many emotions. When he came out of the water, he embraced me for what seemed like a very long time. All I could do was weep and thank God for His mercies and blessings. Later that week, we all piled into our minivan and made the journey to San Antonio. There were a lot of tears shed that day, but also we were thankful for the miraculous time we had shared.

In November 2009, I deployed to Iraq. TJ had returned to San Antonio, his mother having returned from her deployment, and he was well into the school year. I called him when I could and discovered that our phone calls were vastly different than before. There was a connection now that was not present in the past. He was always quick to let me know that he was still doing well in school and that he was on top of his work. I came home on mid-tour leave in February 2010 and was able to have him for the duration. After I returned to Iraq, one night I called him. We spoke about the usual things, but this time he asked me a question that surprised me. He asked if I was scared. TJ knew that I was serving in a company that provided convoy security, which was one of the most dangerous jobs. I explained to him that as a Platoon Sergeant, I did not go on every mission, however, I did have to decide which of my soldiers would go. I told him that I was scared when I was outside the wire, but that I worried more about my soldiers' safety. In fact, I would rather go myself than have them be at risk. I could tell he was trying to contemplate the enormity of what I had said, and shortly after that conversation we ended the call. Due to the drawdown, our tour was cut short, so by mid-July I was home. The building program in Fredericksburg had come a long way in my absence. Many weekends and nights were spent working on the church. TJ would come on his visitation weekends and eagerly assist where he could. He helped put in ceiling tiles and the lights in the sanctuary. He also helped us put the cross on the front of the building. In January 2011, we moved into the new facility. During one visit, there was a mighty move of the Spirit. We had been uncertain how TJ's faith had survived his return home, but now God would give us confirmation that he still had his faith. During this service, people began to shout and praise God. TJ, without prompting, raised his hands to worship. This was completely out of character for the introverted young man. Pastor Steadman, his wife, I and my wife all looked at each other and began to shout. For an average person this was no big deal, but for TJ it was like anyone else running the aisles.

By September 2011, we were ready to have our dedication service. TJ made it a point to be there and participate. Little did any of us know that within a few short weeks, our lives would be forever changed.

The morning of October 25th began as many others. I had awakened to the sound of my alarm and began the process of getting ready for work. Not long after, I heard my phone ring. It was my sister calling me, stating that TJ's mother was with him at the hospital and needed me to call her. My sister worked in San Antonio at the same company as TJ's mother. So I hung up with her and immediately called his mother. She told me he had awakened in the night in pain. Out of character, he was yelling quite a bit, so she called an ambulance. She stated they were saying it was possibly kidney stones and they were looking to release him. This was an odd diagnosis for a fifteen-year-old who had started running cross country track in August and was known to drink water like a fish. I told her I would come to the hospital. During my eighty-mile trek, I called my supervisor in San Antonio and briefed him on what was happening. I was a little nervous as I had only been under him for two weeks. Once I arrived at the hospital, I saw my sister waiting there. She had felt strong in the spirit to come. TJ and his mother were out of the room while they performed a CT scan on him. Nancy and I sat talking, thinking it might be appendicitis or something of that nature. They wheeled TJ into the room and as our eyes met, I could see great excitement and relief in his eyes that I was there. The doctor immediately asked his mother and me to step into an office on the side. As I was active military at the time, I was in my duty uniform. To this day I cannot say why, but the doctor grabbed my hand and began to tell me that TJ had cancer. It had metastasized twice and spread significantly from what they could see, but more extensive testing would need to be done. That would be the longest and most trying day of my life up to that point. After making numerous emotional calls and waiting for hours as testing was being conducted, our prayer was that the news would not be too bad, that perhaps it was limited to the area where it was discovered. As I pondered over all the possibilities, I thought about a conversation I had with TJ as we were taking him to begin the testing. He would be put under since the testing would take considerable time. I was holding his hand and I asked him how he was feeling, if he was scared. He said that he was a little, but that he was more worried about everyone else. I reminded him of our conversation when I was in Iraq, and I told him that was exactly how I felt. He looked at me and I could see that he understood exactly the depth of what I had told him. I told him no matter what, to hold onto his faith. He nodded in agreement.

Later that evening around 6 pm, the doctor came in to let us know the test results. He stated, "The initial tumor formed in his right testicle, metastasized into his abdomen creating a large mass there; it too had metastasized and had spread tumors to both lungs, his kidneys, his liver, his lower left leg and to his brain." He was at Stage 4. The plan for treatment would begin immediately, first by removing the affected testicle and starting a regimen of chemotherapy and radiation. He would be in the hospital for up to four weeks initially; the overall treatment would likely span for over a year. His surgery went well and they quickly began the chemotherapy. The marker used to test for improvement was his beta-hCG level. According to the National Cancer Institute website, beta-hCG is "*a hormone found in the blood and urine during pregnancy. It may also be found in higher than normal amounts in patients with some types of cancer, including testicular, ovarian, liver, stomach, and lung cancers, and in other disorders. Measuring the amount of beta-hCG in the blood or urine of cancer patients may help to diagnose cancer and find out how well cancer treatment is working. Beta-hCG is* a type of tumor marker. Also called beta-human chorionic gonadotropin."[1] His levels were extremely high at this time. As word began to spread, many churches in Austin, San Antonio, and Fredericksburg began to pray. Over the next few weeks, we began to get reports of massive amounts of people across the United States and Canada who were praying for TJ. From New Zealand all the way to Europe, a global effort of prayer had erupted. He was amazed and humbled that all of these people he had never met were praying for him. As more reports of prayer came in, the results from his treatment began to come in also. His beta-hCG levels were not just coming down, they were plummeting. His doctor could not believe how quickly he was bouncing back. We knew exactly what was happening: God was intervening. For the next several months we continued to receive miraculous reports of his progress.

His doctor even admitted to Pastor Steadman and me that TJ's turnaround was a certified miracle. He had been treating pediatric oncology patients for over thirty years, was renowned throughout the world as a premiere expert in his field. This made us rejoice! I would frequently go between Fredericksburg and San Antonio, coming back to testify of the great things God was doing.

---

[1] National Cancer Institute. (2018, March 14). *NCI Dictionary of Cancer Terms*. Retrieved from National Cancer Institute: https://www.cancer.gov/publications/dictionaries/cancer-terms/def/beta-hcg

So well was his treatment working, they had completely diminished his radiation treatment. By April, the doctor was telling us to make plans for the summer, because TJ would be ready to go. He had just turned sixteen and his Aunt Nancy had promised him a red car and would pay for his driving lessons to get his driver's license. There would be a three-week period from his last radiation treatment to another full gambit of testing to allow the effects to take hold. Within two weeks, TJ began to see colors, have headaches and at one point lost feeling in his left arm. We immediately took him in to see his doctor. The news had turned grim, TJ was again Stage 4 and all the tumors had returned. We were informed another specialist from St. Jude's Children's Hospital would join the team and take charge of the next phase of treatment. Our summer plans were cancelled. We would spend the next four months in the hospital, watching as massive amounts of chemotherapy and radiation ravaged his young body. This was a time I began to worry about his faith, how TJ would hold out with such a turn. It seemed like the young man who had prayed and trusted God to take care of his mother and father in a combat zone was now getting shortchanged on miracles.

At the end of August, the doctors informed us there was nothing else that could be done. Two weeks later, TJ returned to the hospital for what would be the last time. As the days passed, I felt guilty. It was like I had told my son about this magnificent God that could do all things, only to have it end like this. I was too scared to ask about his faith. One day towards the end, his brothers Jacob and Daniel were finally able to come into his room and visit. This was due to his low immune system. Little Daniel, now three years old, walked over to his bed and asked to pray for his big brother. We all joined him, even TJ. The next week, his team of doctors came by to see him. A heated discussion began between TJ and his doctors about what was going to happen next. The doctors were trying to tell TJ there was no hope, but he refused to believe them. I remember making eye contact with my sister, wanting to shout hallelujah, because we knew what TJ meant. There was hope, not hope in mortal means but in the supernatural means. Frustrated, the doctors took me to another room and tried to convince me to make him understand that all was lost, there was no hope. In anger, I slammed my fist on the table and declared that I would not go and tell my son there was no hope, that his hope was not in their methods, but in a higher and greater power. I told them I would not destroy the only hope he had left. The lead doctor, a man of faith, suddenly realized that TJ was holding on to his faith. He said, "You're right, we are wrong to try and take that away." Later that night, TJ slipped into a coma, never to wake again. Two days later, the night before he passed, I remember praying to God, and asking Him to take the miracle we had asked for to heal TJ, and use it to help heal his friends and family. The next day, on October 1, 2012, Tyler Jesse Moore passed away.

My reflection on the events immediately after his passing are quite vague. All I can say is the pain was immeasurable. I do remember finally getting some time alone a few weeks after his passing, and I finally had a very straightforward discussion with our Creator. With weeping, yelling, moaning, waling or whatever sounds I could muster, I cried out to God. At that moment in my life, it was the most honest prayer I'd ever had with God. Formality was out the door, this was a raw emotional conversation taking place. I can testify with all certainty that honest prayer is what God wants from us. He's not interested in our structured prayer in our most desperate hour, but our sincerest and most honest prayer. Only when we open up completely can He begin the process of healing. I simply stated that I needed Him to take away my question of why. Why him? Because as a father, I understood there were many times I had to take things from my children, and regardless of how good of a reason I gave them, all they wanted was what I was taking away. Just like those children, I told my heavenly Father that no matter why He had taken TJ, as a child of God, no reason would matter to me, I simply wanted my son. So again I pleaded for Him to please take away the question "why?" in my heart. In that moment, I felt a peace I had not felt in a long time. It was a sliver of light in a very dark time, but it was exactly what I needed, relief from asking why. I knew the process of healing would be long, but that moment gave me hope that God would deliver on His promise found in Deuteronomy 31:6 (KJV) *"Be strong and of a good courage, ...he will not fail thee, nor forsake thee."*

I was transferred to Austin in 2013, returning to New Life Church in Austin. We have seen many major transitions. I retired from the military after twenty-eight years, my son Jacob is now in high school and Daniel is in third grade, having received the Holy Ghost and been baptized at Vacation Bible School in 2017. Jacob received the Spirit in 2010 at General Conference and I baptized him upon our return. The journey has been long, yet continues. As a family, we have grown together, always reflecting on TJ, sharing memories and celebrating his life. In 2017, I volunteered to take over as coordinator for the Grief Share program at our church. Since we began, God has used my testimony to help others find peace in their faith during their time of loss. We have managed to help them understand that maintaining and strengthening their relationship with the Creator during this dark time is vital to healing. As I pursue my call to be an evangelist, I pray that God continues to use my testimony to reach others, providing the promised hope, but most of all fulfilling His word that states, *"And the peace of God, which passeth all understanding, shall keep your hearts and minds through Christ Jesus." Philippians 4:7(KJV)*

Vida Mia & Sarai Jiménez

The Jiménez Family

CHAPTER 6

Sarai Jimenez

At the age of seventeen, I was diagnosed with Myasthenia Gravis. It is a disease that attacks the muscles and the nerves that control them. It kept me from doing the regular things in life, even the smallest things you don't ever think about. Myasthenia Gravis took so much away from me as I was growing up and becoming an adult. It took away the joy of playing in any sport, the joy of playing in the school band and just living a normal life. By the time I had reached my early twenties, I had started living life without fear and I threw caution to the wind. To me, although at times I felt physically weak, life was too amazingly exciting to take it easy. That didn't seem to bother me since I was living the single life and more so not having to surrender anything to anyone. I was without God and thought everything I was getting in the world was making up for any unhappiness that I would come across. I went from having an unhealthy relationship with a man to being alone. I thought that my happiness was predicated on a sinful relationship with a man who ultimately caused so much pain, loneliness, and heartbreak. At that point in life I was constantly thinking, *what am I doing so wrong to keep getting hurt and used?* I soon found myself alone again, playing the single life game. I promised myself that this time it would be different, but I kept seeking happiness all in the wrong places with all the wrong people. I could never find it, nor understand why I couldn't obtain it when everyone around me seemed so happy and full of life. I needed something more and I wasn't giving up until I found it. I was thinking that having friends and going out would just make up for it. I started going out with a group of friends who, like me, lived carefree and reckless, drinking their sorrows away. Thinking I was loved by those who surrounded me, I went seeking something I didn't know would end up causing me more pain than ever before. One night, a couple of friends and I decided to go out to a concert and drink ourselves happy. We all ended up sleeping over one of their homes because it was very late for me to drive home. I thought I was safe because I was amongst friends, but I came across the worst feeling of fear any woman could face. The husband of one of my girlfriends thought I was her and in the middle of the night he came into the room where I was sleeping. As I suddenly woke up, a chill ran down my spine, feeling a man's body clutching mine. But even then, God knew my purpose and protected me. I asked him what he was doing. His answer was, "Oh I thought you were my wife." At that moment I knew I was in the wrong place and just needed to go home. So, I did. With tears in my eyes, without saying a word, I drove home. As I drove in the lonely night, my tears kept flowing and I couldn't help but cry out to the God, who at this point protected me throughout a life without Him. I truly did not deserve it, yet His grace was sufficient for me. I remember thanking Him even though I didn't live for Him. I thanked Him anyway because anything worse could have happened and it didn't. Once again I found myself all alone without any family support. I hardly communicated with them because I thought I was better off without them and could handle my life by myself. So, I then started working at a restaurant closer to home and went back to my old ways, seeking happiness apart from God. But this time I had decided not to drink nor sleep over anyone's home, for I had learned my lesson the hard way. These subtle adjustments in my life did not bring the peace I was looking for. I was still missing something, and I just couldn't figure out what it was. I would still come home with an emptiness that would have me wondering how I could live a fulfilling life and if true happiness would ever be mine. I worked and went out and worked some more, but the same old same old, I was aimlessly in a rut with no direction, slowly losing hope with each passing day.

    One day out of the blue, my boss asked me if I could help his partner at a different location that would pay me far better than what I was making at the time. So I decided to try something new and meet new people. Little did I know that I would meet the love of my life, and eventually marry this man as well.

Rafael and I met in the summer of 2008 and he, along with my coworkers, spent our free time together eating, drinking and just hanging out. At this point Rafael and I were just friends, but as the months went by we became more than friends. I could see in a short period of time that I was falling in love with him. I finally had found someone who treated me so different from any other man I had known. When I was with Rafael I was never lonely or sad. He brought joy and happiness in ways that I thought were not possible, so I took a leap of faith and together we decided that living together was what both of us wanted and needed from each other. Again, without fear of living in sin or any thought of feeling like I was in the wrong, I made a decision to go against God's law and His word. To me, everything felt great and perfect, for I was with a man who fulfilled my every need.

The year of 2009 came around and Rafael and I were still working for the same boss at the same restaurant, but I decided to quit and become a stay-at-home wife. We then decided to make it official and tie the knot with a beautiful church wedding, and my dream of living happily ever after was starting to unfold. This man wanted to take me to the altar and I was more than happy to become his wife. As we continued to plan our wedding, his father became very ill and had to go through surgery. That immediately postponed our wedding plans and wedding. February came around and I was home one day with my mother-in-law, and at this point I would sleep so much that it was starting to worry everyone. Something in me said to take a pregnancy test. I thought, *you have nothing to lose. What's the worse that can happen?* I mean, I was so afraid of not becoming pregnant, for that was what I wanted to be complete with Rafael. In the back of my mind I could hear the voices of the neurologists saying I could never become pregnant because of Myasthenia Gravis. Once again fear came into my heart and felt horrible, and I said to myself I could never have a family.

But, God knew exactly what He was doing. Even though I didn't serve or live for Him, His grace seemed to find me somehow. So, I took that pregnancy test and minutes of anxiousness overwhelmed me. It was POSITIVE. I was shocked, I was in silent mode. I WAS PREGNANT and I couldn't speak nor had words, for the home test had given me an answer I had hoped for. I ran to the kitchen where my mother-in-law was and stood there for minutes, not knowing how to tell her. Should I tell her or call Rafael at work? I was just so excited that she knew then what was going on, and without me saying a word she asked in Spanish, "Estás embarazada (are you pregnant)?" I replied, "How did you know?" Well, I leaped for joy, but then stopped jumping, thinking it could harm the baby. Crazy, I know.

I called Rafael at work and went speechless, and he then also knew from that moment that I was pregnant.

Rafael was so excited, he came home from work. As we proceeded with doctor's visits and follow-ups with the neurologist, fear and doubt still troubled my mind. This could not possibly happen, or even worse, what if the baby was born with physical problems? They monitored me very well, but in the middle of my second trimester Rafael and I started having problems. Yes, the man whom I loved with all my heart and I were going through a rough and bumpy road. I couldn't explain what went wrong and I couldn't explain where our lives were heading as a couple, much less know if we'd be together. We were so desperate to find out what was going wrong with our lives and how to find a solution. We wanted our relationship to work and we were willing to do anything possible to save it. Even more so since a baby was on the way. We were in total desperation mode and were willing to try anything. As embarrassing as this is for me to admit, we consulted and paid for a witch to solve our problems. Yes, it's sad what we do when we have no guidance of the one true king (Jesus Christ). We wasted our money and nothing was ever really resolved. We still had problems and I moved in with my mom till I was six months pregnant. We soon decided that either we would make it work for the best interest of the baby or just end our relationship. Rafael was a very caring and loving father and wanted the best for his baby. He never left me alone, despite our troubles. There were moments where I didn't want to see him nor speak to him nor have him anywhere near me. Whether it was witchcraft or just simply life, all I knew was that I was losing what I had always hoped for and I was terrified.

We then decided to move to East End because he got offered a job opportunity that he couldn't pass up. Working together (seven months pregnant) was not an ideal situation, but we were trying our best to stay together. What kept us from going crazy? At the moment I didn't know, but my God did. And you may ask why all the explanation? Because He already had an answer to our problems and a future miracle that I knew nothing about. See, through it all I had ignored the fact that it was God at all times working in some way in my life, but I was too dull spiritually to realize it. Shortly after that, I met the Manchacks. Pastor David Manchack and his wife Janice were pastoring a Pentecostal church close by. They soon started coming in almost every Sunday to eat at the restaurant we worked at. They left a card from the church and right then and there I knew just where to start my search to fill that empty space in my heart. Weeks went by before I actually decided to give them a visit. I was actually raised Pentecostal, so I knew what I was going to encounter when I visited. At this time I was almost eight months pregnant and had stopped working. This made it so much easier to attend church more regularly, and the Lord began to deal with me. At this point of my pregnancy I was very tired and started swelling up in my hands, feet, and my face. I could not sleep in my own bed because I had breathing problems and a shortness of breath. This is where things become more intense.

As I got closer to labor, I found myself sleeping on the couch in a sitting position almost every night. One morning I woke up and started my day, but something didn't feel right. The baby had not moved all morning and boy, was she an active baby. So, I started the day not paying much attention to the issue. Something still made me call the nurse and ask if I could come in and get checked or should I just let it pass. She suggested that I drink orange juice and that would make her move. By this time, it was getting close to the evening and still the baby did not move. The orange juice was not doing it and nothing was making her move. I was scared and tried to keep calm, but that was easier said than done. The night came around and once again I found myself sitting on the couch because I couldn't breathe well lying down. All through the night I was more worried about the baby than anything else. I was frightened, and just hoped for the best. Morning came around and I was swollen from head to toe and felt horrible. I was soon taken to the OBGYN about thirty minutes away from home. And then, the worst came and I was rushed to the hospital, not knowing what was going on but always told everything would be fine.

I was lost and terrified and no one would tell me what was going on with me or my baby. All I was told was that we'd have to go to the hospital because there was better equipment there than at the doctors' office. Still frightened and hoping for the best, I received the news that changed my mind, heart and all that was in me. I just wanted some way, somehow find a way to feel certain everything was truly going to be okay. See, Myasthenia Gravis had done its thing and without notice, I wasn't able to breathe well. It had nothing to do with being pregnant and overweight, but rather because I was losing strength to breathe on my own. The rest of my body was losing strength as well and I was at a complete loss. When the doctors said, "Your baby isn't receiving oxygen and we need to intubate you immediately," my heart sank. I was horrified but had to trust the doctors because they had experience in these matters and knew just what to do. I cried and cried scared half to death and fearing the worst. Every family member who was close was notified, and I'm sure Mom called many others, because all I remember was that everyone that I knew was there. We found ourselves in ICU and on life support. My husband and mom were told that I'd have to get transferred to Little Rock to UAMS Hospital because they had the best neurologists in the area and would take very good care of me. So, they proceeded to take me off the ventilator, and then more horrifying news presented itself. Doctors told my husband and my mom to pray for the best because it was about an hour's drive without the ventilator and it would be touch and go all the way.

    I, on the other hand, was so scared and cried and prayed the only way I knew how. I cried out from the bottom of my heart and asked God to help me out of the situation I was in. I didn't want to lose my firstborn, nor did I want to leave her alone. In the ambulance with just the oxygen tank and the paramedics, I asked as best that I could if everything still looked okay with the baby, but they just couldn't assure me of anything. See, through this whole pregnancy, I never found myself so broken and lost. I knew my only way out would be God and my miracle would be done and given by Him. I then had realized that my life and my daughter's life were in His hands and that there was nothing anyone could do but Him.

We arrived at the hospital and were soon rushed back into ICU and I found myself on the ventilator once again and monitored by doctors 24/7, and nurses and an OBGYN as well. Family flew in from Salt Lake City, Utah and some from hours away. Friends and family gathered for days and prayed and hoped for the best. Days kept going by and soon turned into a week and then a week and a half and nothing yet. Through it all, I was also getting treated with apheresis, which would be a total of five treatments in total but couldn't be done one day after another. They'd have to skip one day and so on. So, by this time everyone was still praying that I get enough strength so that I could breathe on my own and give the oxygen necessary to my unborn child. The Manchacks had the church raise money and handed it to Rafael for he had never left my side and couldn't or didn't want to work. It was a complete blessing to have met them, for I know they prayed and prayed for our little miracle.

Days kept going by, and all I can remember was my husband crying and my mom and brother Gary had been there for many days. I was sedated most of the time and all I can recall was that I wasn't able to speak, but I was able to write. I was given a note pad and that was my way of communicating with everyone. I kept praying and hoping for the best. I soon felt my little life in me move, even though being sedated and drowsy for days and dealing with the intubation and painful tubes. I gradually started to feel better and was conscious and felt the baby and started to ask if I could be taken off the ventilator. But no, it wasn't time. Little did they know, after weeks of being there and getting treated, my God decided to intervene and produce the miracle that only He could. Yes, I started contracting and everyone got alarmed, thinking I wasn't ready. At this point in a pregnancy coupled with the physical issues I had, they believed that only one of us was going to live through this ordeal. It would either be me or my baby that would die that day. My mom and my husband were informed to make a decision as to who was going to live, and they would proceed accordingly. Scary I know, but God had a better plan for us. The Lord didn't want to cause pain, but was trying to reach me through a tough situation, and knew I would seek Him if He touched what I most wanted in life, my little baby. It was then that I placed everything in His hands, and in doing so I was then taken off the ventilator and placed in a regular room. I remember the nurses coming in and out, but in no time I kept contracting and was then transferred to Labor and Delivery. I was dilated and the baby was coming. Doctors were confused by how all of a sudden one minute I'm on the ventilator and the next I'm off of it, and in labor. They decided to go through with the delivery. Not only did I feel confident of having her naturally but I was certain in my heart that God would pull me through as well. The doctors got ready for plan B in case I wouldn't be able to deliver normally, and had the cesarean room ready. But NO, I was ready to have my baby and excited to finally meet her. Everyone stood with me in the room and waited to meet her as well. Everyone was scared too, thinking I could lose all my strength and not be able to push her out and become extremely weak after having her. But see that's where I knew that the strength wouldn't come from me but from God.

    I then found myself having my little miracle, but that wasn't all joy and happiness. No, something was wrong, but once again no one would tell me anything. Baby girl wasn't breathing nor responding. There was silence in the room and all I would ask was, "Can I have my baby? Can I see her?" But the doctors kept working on me while working on her. Ten minutes of silence were the longest of my entire life. Then, my miracle baby cried and I was able to hear her voice and see her beautiful face.

    This momma got to hold the miracle God had sent her. We all rejoiced and welcomed my baby ("Vida Mia" -- literally "My Life" in Spanish) into the world in November of 2009. Vida was then sent to the NICU, since she had inhaled some liquid and had to be monitored. But again, my God showed Himself and my baby girl was tougher and stronger than the doctors had thought possible. They said she was the healthiest baby in the NICU when originally, they thought she wouldn't make it because of all the setbacks she had to endure.

Days later we were discharged and ready to meet the world.

Eight years down the road and two more babies, I find myself serving the Lord and thanking Him for the many miracles and blessings He has filled me with. Eight years later, doctors to this day remember what happened and can't explain how I overcame that crisis of Myasthenia Gravis. We know how. God almighty and mercy made it happen. Not only one baby but I was blessed with three in all. Through all of this and all these years, I keep praying for my husband who isn't converted, but he too has seen God's mercy and hand upon our family. I'm more than certain that he is thankful for our family because we thought we would never be able to see a child of our own. God showed me that in the middle of that huge storm, He never left my side He never forsook me, just like His word says.

How can I not serve Him? How could I not be grateful for all that He brought me through just to get to Him? God had a purpose in my life and has a purpose in the lives of my family. Maybe not now, but He always seems to appear at the right time and at the right precise moment. I have learned through my walk in Him that He allows many things to occur, not to punish us, but rather as a wakeup call from the life we were once living apart from Him. He has always had better plans for us than we do for ourselves. He also knew what I'd be blessed with in the future and He knew and saw my life ahead. So to this day I keep serving the Lord. I keep walking in faith and not by sight. It is very hard, but you know what they say, without a test there wouldn't be a testimony. This is mine and I pray and hope it touches someone and encourages them to take that step of faith and let Him walk us through the storm. Blessings from the Jimenez family.

The Sandoval Family

CHAPTER 7

Pastor Adiel Sandoval

My name is Adiel Sandoval Bustamante, also known as Adiel S. Medina. My last name changed when I was adopted in the United States of America.

My Beginning

My parents, Pedro Sandoval and Leonila Bustamante, were long time evangelist pastors since the 1940s in the Mexican states of Sinaloa, Sonora and Baja California. I was born in Caborca, Sonora in 1974. When my parents were old, and because of circumstances of need, in 1989 they decided to send their three youngest boys to the United States to live with two of their older sons who lived in the state of California. I was fourteen years old at the time.

Border Crossing

We tried crossing into the United States from Baja, California. For about a month we traveled through the cities of Mexicali, Tecate and Tijuana when I and my two brothers finally crossed into the United States. In 1991, during summer vacations and after completing my junior year in high school, my younger brother and I were adopted by a very kind couple from the church we were baptized in. Their names were Jose Natividad Medina and Sofia Araujo. They didn´t have children at that time and God placed it in their hearts to take us, not only to live with them but also to adopt us as well. Before that, they spoke with our parents and our older brothers, and my parents agreed to sign the adoption documents. My parents felt that it was part of God´s plan to better prepare us for our future in Him.

Great Opportunities

When I arrived in the United States, I studied three years in high school, where I learned the English language, and graduated in 1992 with a scholarship. I had several options of universities because of the good grades I had received and also because of the support of my adoptive parents. The option I chose brought great joy to my adoptive parents. I decided on furthering my education at a Bible college. The Apostolic Bible College of the Apostolic Assembly was my choice to pursue the calling God had placed upon my heart since

I was a child. This decision would help me to follow in my parents' footsteps.

When I was finishing Bible college there was an opportunity to work part time at the International Headquarters of the Apostolic Assembly. It was a dream job of sorts for any young man or young woman who desired to serve God, and truthfully it kind of just fell in my lap. I started working part time as a translator, then writing and designing for Sunday School quarterlies. I was finally working full time with a lot of great opportunities to grow in every area of my life, including spiritually. When God called the brother, who oversaw all the pre-press and printing, to become a pastor, I was assigned that great responsibility and I went at it with everything I had.

My 'Legal' Situation

When I was adopted all I was given was a Social Security card and number to use for studying and as a legal document to travel in the United States, but it did not change my legal status. We tried to legalize my status in the United States through adoption, but it didn´t proceed because I was already sixteen years old when I was adopted. We tried through a petition of religious work, but it remained in limbo without very many options. During summer vacations from Bible college, I used to work in construction with a friend from the church and one time while crossing an immigration checkpoint inside the United States, even after showing the legal papers I had, I was processed for deportation. But after making a call to my adoptive parents, the immigration officer in charge decided to let me go home, but he never cancelled the order of deportation and sent me a court order citation to the Immigration Department in Los Angeles, CA.

We started an annual citation process and we hired a lawyer, who was helping us to legalize my status. On one of the citations, our lawyer told us that I had to leave the country, because there wasn't anything more to do, but nothing happened and I was not deported that year. The following year, it seemed that the immigration process was improving. I went to court, but the lawyer helping my case suffered a mild heart attack the same day, and we didn't know it. I went before the judge and he decided to sign a deportation order because he said that the deportation document that was against me since I crossed an immigration checkpoint years back was still open, and it was never cancelled during the process. While exiting the United States, I signed a voluntary deportation document in 1999.

God Knows What He is Doing

For many people, a deportation from the United States might seem a loss instead of a victory, but God had everything planned and His plans are always higher and better than ours. By the time I was deported I was twenty-four years old and I was blessed more than I deserved. I had completed three years of studies in Bible college and I had worked for about seven years at the International Headquarters of the Apostolic Assembly. I know now that God had orchestrated everything to happen exactly as it did, and He was only setting things up for greater blessings. I learned a lot in Bible college. It was a live-in college and it had a lot of great experienced professors. During my working years I also learned a lot from my co-workers and the institution´s directors. Besides, the work I did was constantly about the Bible and its great good for society. I also met Bro. George Pantages, whom I admired for his calling and dedication to God and His work. I learned a lot from my pastors in the United States. I somehow was always close to them and took advantage of their trust for my personal growth. Especially Pastor Sam Valverde, who was my pastor for many years and my employer at the headquarters. Working in the Christian Education Department gave me the opportunity to visit many states in the US and that helped me in my ministerial development.

I remember that when I was being deported, the personnel at the deportation office in Los Angeles, a very kind black officer, who filled the deportation order, when seeing my certificates of study and where I was working, told me – "We shouldn`t be deporting you. "Here in the United States of America, we need more people like you."

I left the country with a mentality that a chapter was being closed in my life, I wasn't feeling disappointed towards God, not while leaving. I felt a peace from God, that there was something new ahead. I didn´t know what it was, but I trusted that God is always in control above everything else.

How I Met My Wife

There was a young girl that I knew since I was very young. We were born in the same city and I found out that she had a petition before God for more than a year. She was continually asking God for a husband and God had already confirmed to her through a prophetic word that He had a husband reserved for her. Even though she didn't know who she was praying for, she had a specific list about her future husband. This young man would have to truly love God, for if he loved the Lord in that manner, loving her would be a piece of cake. Her list also included that he would specifically come from the United States, that he would be a musician, and of course, that she would be attracted to him. She was clear that a lack of being handsome was not an issue.

Now, smiling, she testifies to the younger generation to ask God specifically because she forgot to ask God that he would be an American citizen, not one deported from the United States.

When I was deported back to Mexico, it had been eleven years from the last time I had seen her. I thought she was already married because she was so beautiful, and I used to secretly admire her when we were younger. When I found out she wasn't married, I decided to visit her by first asking her father's permission to let me come to their home. Her father gave me the green light and I started to visit her. My future father-in-law, Julian Diaz, was my father's employer for many years, so both families knew each other very well. Even on my mother-in-law's side, Rosalva Castillo, the families have known each other for a long time and the friendship goes back to more than half a century. Our renewed friendship turned into love and when I asked her to marry me, surprisingly she said yes. It made me the happiest and most blessed man on earth.

The Story Goes Back to 1936

My father and my wife's grandparents met since my father got converted and baptized in Jesus' name. When my father converted to Christ, he was a professional musician. He used to play in the orchestra of Pedro Infante's father, one of the most famous Mexican actors of all time. Every once in a while, he also got together with Pedro to show off his musical talent. When he gave his heart to the Lord and was water baptized, he left that kind of life behind and went back to work in the fields. While he was working one day, an Apostolic couple invited him to come to the Apostolic Church. Because he had been evangelized by a German missionary, he knew nothing about the Oneness doctrine. He had been baptized in the titles Father, Son, and Holy Ghost, but after receiving a revelation in a dream of the baptism in Jesus' Name he was re-baptized according to Acts 2:38. The pastor who baptized him left the state because he was in another Oneness movement and went back home. So, this couple led my father to the Apostolic Church in Mexico. He was ordained as a minister and the Church sent him to open new works in the state of Sonora. That separated my father from my wife's grandparents for more than forty years, and then they met again in the city where my wife and I were born. Now, my wife and I happily ask if they made some kind of a deal about their offspring the moment they met and became friends back in the 1930s. For sure, it must have been a very great deal.

The Pastorship

In 1993, my father died while I was still studying in Bible college. When I was deported my mom was the only one living, so I returned to my mother's house with the purpose of pursuing God's calling in my life. I was a deacon for four years in the US and not being able to become an ordained minister because of my legal situation. In Mexico I continued as a deacon, and after another four years I was ordained as a minister. God gave me the opportunity to become a pastor in 2011 in the Apostolic Organization I am now serving. In this time of reacquainting myself with the church in Mexico, I always had seen God's love, His hand, His power and His protection all along the process. My wife and I have acknowledged that God is faithful to His promises, and that when things don't go according to our own goals and dreams, He will always have a much better perspective of what is happening and a perfect purpose in everything. All His ways are perfect and positive, even when our numbers and our experiences are negative. I have experienced His promises in my life over and over even when I don't seem to love Him as He deserves and as I should; the promise that to those who love God, everything turns out for good.

God's Surprises

God's surprises are the best ones. He cares for His people, He is the best Father and Protector of the universe. If you are going through a most difficult and desperate situation, you can be sure that God will keep you in His loving arms and you will see His beautiful glory in the midst of it all. There are surprises He has reserved for you, just hold on and stay in Him.

To the unmarried youth that read this testimony, my wife and I tell you that God has a perfect princess for you, a perfect prince, do not despair. Do not go ahead of God, do not worry, wait in God and He will work the best for you. He knows your life and has a perfect one for you, there is no doubt about it.

God blessed us with two beautiful princesses, Angie and Hannah, after we had gone through a period of infertility for six long years. It literally took a miracle for my wife to conceive. It was only after a prophetic word from God that our first daughter was born. The Lord went out of His way to make sure we understood that for God, "timing" is everything.

Thirteen years had gone by after being deported, and only then we applied for a US tourist visa. To our shock we received it, even though I had gone through a deportation. God truly knows how to take pain and heartbreak, and make it into something beautiful! We are now currently working as full-time pastors in Nogales, Sonora Mexico in a congregation that is willing to impact and reach the community for God. THE BEST IS YET TO COME!

I thank Evangelist George Pantages for the opportunity to be part of this book.

God Bless You Abundantly!

Pastor Anthony Martinez

2011 Western States H.S. Championship

Street Ministry - Oxnard, CA

CHAPTER 8

Pastor Anthony Martinez

I'm reminded of a conversation I had with a wonderful man that the Lord had put in my life to help mentor me. His name was Pastor Edmond L. Dyess. He took his finger and started to draw out what he was about to tell me. He said that life is like a circle, you have a starting point and you go on in struggles, experiences, highs and lows and you come around to build upon those things. As he began to finish the other half of the circle, he said that eventually you come back to where you started. The point is: how big is your circle? As you grow the circle grows larger in learning, faith becomes an effect to widen the circle. But through each growth spurt you will come back to where you started. Then he started to make small circles as fast as he could go to explain how many go through vicious cycles going through the same things over and over again. He then brought his finger to his ear and said, "It drives them "crazy."

These words have become very meaningful to me as I find myself where I'm at now. After thirty years since I left the city where I was born and raised, I was brought back and led by the Lord to do something I never thought was planned for me. There was a long time where if you had told me I would be here, I would laugh and say you were out of your mind. My claim was, "I will never go back there." But here I am. The complete circle, only now not the same man that I was when I left. The experiences, growth, faith building struggles that the Lord has brought us through have made what we are facing ahead possible."

When the author, George Pantages asked me to share with you my experiences, I thought that this would be a way for me to say, "Thank you, Lord, for all that you've done for me." As the circle was being completed in my life, God's love, grace, mercy and everything that was needed was poured out on me. We serve a very patient Father. Since I can remember the Lord's Spirit has always moved on me. There was placed in me a sensitive heart for the touch of God. Growing up in an Apostolic Church was a big part of that. Remembering as a boy my grandfather preaching, it always amazed me how the Lord moved on His people. When the anointing would fall on the preacher and the congregation, I would run to be in the middle of it all. Watching every movement, every response just mesmerized me. Brothers and sisters falling out, dancing, being slain in the Spirit of the Lord, demons being cast out, and I wanted all of it.

I was what was known as a latch key kid. This was in the 60's and 70's. It was just my mother and I. There was no father or siblings. Mom worked at the hospital across the street from the apartments where we lived. She would have to leave me alone at the house. There were some fearful days, lonely times. But even then I would sing and worship the Lord and he would touch me. I was so young yet I would be weeping and moved by God's love and compassion. I understand that now, but for a child it was a sweet comfort. I remember thinking that there was something different about me. The difference made me think myself strange. This seemed to be the beginning of the call of God on my life. I also believe that the devil also saw the same. And so began the plan to distort, warp and ruin what God had started in me. Being young and alone can leave you an open target for anyone and anything by the carnal and the ungodly. The enemies' plan consisted much of both from those closest to me and started much physical and mental abuse. This plan included distorting my love for what I thought was pure and precious. My view of God's church and His people began to be a very low outlook.

It started with friends from school along with their older brothers, family members who took advantage of me sexually. The details I will leave out. No need to get into the specifics. This stole any and all trust I had for anyone. Shame and rage welled up inside that would soon be revealed in my behavior. I started to get into fights at school and became an introvert. As I got older, the rage became uncontrollable. I was confused about how God could let this happen to me. I reasoned that since my mom was the only person in my family going to church that God shouldn't let this happen to us. How could He allow this? These thoughts gave rise to bitterness, and dealing with it would become my lifelong struggle.

The deeper heartache came from the place I thought would be my refuge, the church. It was there I sought protection, but sadly I found no refuge. Between the ages of ten and fourteen I saw things in church that resulted in what I call spiritual trauma. I witnessed a fist fight between two ministers in the church restroom and thought, "Aren't these the men that pray for me and my friends and family to be blessed?" On a different occasion an evangelist came to town to hold a tent revival. I was sitting in the audience when I saw a young man from my church walk up the middle aisle and stop at the platform. He began yelling and raised his hand in an obscene gesture toward a pastor seated there. In a heartbeat, the pastor jumped out of his chair and off the platform on the young man and they began to exchange blows. Instead of pulling them apart and settling the situation, more preachers joined in the fight and it became a free-for-all. I remember my mother trying to cover my eyes, but I wiggled out of her grasp and saw the whole thing. But brawling ministry wasn't the only problem I saw with men who were supposedly called of God.

I was raised by a single, divorced mother at a time when divorce was unacceptable in general and almost unheard of in the church. Divorced women were considered to have loose morals and my mother was not an exception. I love my mother deeply and she acted in what she thought were my best interests, but she sometimes did not set adequate boundaries with the men of God she sought help from. I recall married ministers coming to our house alone and making advances toward my mother, one even suggested that they pray in her room. I remember being sent to my room and hearing my mother arguing with this man of God. As a child (and even now) I couldn't reconcile the God that I was hearing about in songs and sermons with the actions of some of the leaders of the church. I developed a distorted view of the church and decided that it was not the place for me. I fought a losing battle with my mother to stay home and eschew all things Apostolic.

By the grace of God and the prayers of my mother, I made it to adolescence without becoming an atheist. I attended Youth Camp and received the Holy Ghost and was baptized in Jesus' name. I never saw my mom so happy. God was bringing healing into my heart, and although I still battled with feelings of anger, I also felt His sweet Spirit moving in me. All seemed to be looking up, when in my sophomore year of high school my mother was diagnosed with terminal cancer. Before the end of the school year, my mother was dead. I was devastated, I felt so alone. I had extended family that loved me, but my mother was my whole life and I didn't know how to handle her loss. I lashed out at family that tried to help me and they were at a loss as to how to reach me. Finally one of my cousins suggested I be sent to the Christian high school in Stockton, California.

While at Stockton, the Lord blessed me. I saw and experienced things I could not have imagined in my home church. I met men and women who truly knew God and walked with Him in a way that inspired me to do the same. I was introduced to men who saw my anger and frustration and felt a deep burden for me. They earned my respect and love through their patience and love for me. It was at Stockton where I first felt the call to preach the Gospel of Jesus Christ. I preached my first sermon when I was fifteen, and God moved in a way that confirmed to me that I was called to preach. After high school I took a few classes at Western Apostolic Bible College, but dropped out in my first year. I was young and arrogant and thought I could work for the Lord on my own terms. I was wrong. I returned home and came face to face with myself and my unresolved feelings of shame and anger.

At home I reverted to what I was taught as a child, attend church and pray. Unfortunately, this was not enough to overcome the emotional and spiritual forces coming against me. Shortly after leaving Stockton, I gave up on church and God altogether. I fell into darkness so deep that I was sure God would want nothing more to do with me. I was wrong. God in His great mercy kept calling me back to Him, there was no place I could go to escape His call. On three separate occasions He saved me from death, and even though I wasn't living for Him, I knew that He was the one who saved me. I eventually arrived at a place where I had nothing, no job, no money, no hope. It was in this place where I finally turned to God and surrendered my life to Him, and He responded with boundless love and mercy.

I had heard of a program called Lifeline Outreach in East L. A. and had family who attended the church. I needed to get away and thought that it would be the right place for me. After speaking with Pastor David Hernandez, he told me that he wouldn't accept me in the program. I was devastated, I thought that God was punishing me for rejecting Him. I was wrong. Bro. Hernandez told me he felt the Lord wanted him to help me and asked me to live in his home. The circle of my life expanded on that day. Brother Hernandez became a mentor to me, and under his leadership I embraced the call of God that I had run from previously. I ministered as a choir director, youth leader, teacher, and ultimately as an ordained minister. I also met my wife and we started our family in East L. A.

I thought that once I became a minister and started working for the Lord that all the pains of my past would simply vanish. I was wrong. There were times when the old pains and shame would overtake me like a flood and crush my spirit. For the next thirty years I remained firm in my faith, and the Lord in His mercy and grace blessed my ministry, but I couldn't understand why I still had so much anger. Dealing with anger that could turn to rage would remain my struggle. It affected my relationships with my wife and children, and if it had not been for the Lord, we never would have made it. I placed my family in spiritually perilous situations because I wouldn't let go of my anger toward those that hurt me. It was in those situations that my Heavenly Father taught me how to trust in Him. He allowed me to go places where my only hope was in Him, and through the years gently chipped away at the pain and bitterness I had been harboring for so long. The Lord began to teach me what real surrender was and how it could change not only my life but the lives of those I love.

When I finally surrendered my hurt and anger to the Lord, I felt renewed. At the time my ministry was on autopilot, I was just going with the flow without a real vision. I was assistant pastor of my church and running the church school, but without the passion I had in the past. My life was changing, I was approaching that time of life when people start to think about slowing down, but the more I surrendered to God the more I felt like there was more He wanted me to do. Then I got a call from the pastor of the church I attended as a child. Back then he was a young minister, a true servant of God that showed kindness to me even when I was at my worst. He asked me to preach a youth revival and I accepted with more than a little hesitation. Being back home stirred up some of the old feelings, but I put my trust in my Heavenly Father and the revival was a success. At the time of this revival the pastor was battling cancer. He told me, "It would be nice to have you back to help with what God has done here." To my amazement, I considered his request seriously and even more amazing, my wife told me that she was willing to leave her hometown if that was where God led me. In all the years I lived away from my hometown, I never considered going back to the place that held so many painful memories. After a lot of prayer and godly counsel, my wife, daughter and I made the move to my hometown. I believe all the highs and lows, all the struggles and changes were to prepare me for where I am now, back where it all started. I have come full circle.

Although I believed that coming back home was the will of God for me, everything didn't fall into place all at once. The pastor who asked me to come home lost his battle with cancer, and the national headquarters of our organization installed a new pastor from out of town. No longer working for the church, I found work through temp agencies for not much more than minimum wage. My wife was forced to keep her job near our old home, eighty miles away, so that we could make ends meet. There were times I wondered if I really had heard from God, and then God opened a door that would lead me down a path I couldn't have imagined.

Through a childhood friend I learned that a nonprofit group was looking for people to work with "at risk" youth. He knew of my work in East L. A. and encouraged me to apply for the job. I was excited about the position, but when I went to the interview I saw I was competing with people who had advanced degrees in social science or counseling or who were already working in the community with different groups. I had experience but no degree, and I was an outsider from L.A. working for temp agencies. I put my trust in God and His will for my life. I got the job. It was a perfect fit for me. At first we walked the streets of the city looking for kids who looked like they were gang affiliated or engaging in harmful activities like drugs and drinking. It was strange to be working in the same streets that I walked as a troubled youth, looking for troubled young people. Through my work I became acutely aware of how far God had brought me. A new desire burned in my soul to know my God and trust Him with my entire being. Little did I know how that desire would be tested.

On my 55th birthday, I was doing my "I'm not an old man" workout when I felt a sharp pain in my chest that radiated down my left arm. I did the sensible thing and ignored it for hours until my wife finally made me go to the doctor. At first all the tests came back negative; no heart attack. In what I considered an overabundance of caution, the doctor made me stay the night and take a stress test in the morning. I failed the test. Since the tests showed no damage to my heart, the doctors were sure that they could fix it by placing a stint in the obstructed artery, which is an outpatient procedure. When they attempted the procedure, however, they discovered that

I needed a triple bypass. I spent five days in the hospital and four months recovering. In the low moments of my recovery I thought, "Lord, did you bring me back here just to die?" I was surprised when His answer was yes. The Lord spoke to me and said that He brought me back to my hometown to die to myself. To finally let go of those things I thought I needed to be a strong man. He said that He would teach me about spiritual healing through my physical recovery. During this time God gave me a new vision and restored the passion I had when I was first filled with His Spirit.

In the years that followed my surgery, I found great fulfillment at work but I had a hard time finding my place in church. I had always been active in the churches I attended, I was everything from a choir director to assistant pastor. The churches I attended in my hometown, however, didn't have a place for me and I became frustrated. Enter a man of God, Brother Gerald Jeffers. Before I met Brother Jeffers, I knew him through his sermons, which affected me deeply. He happened to be preaching at my local church and I had the opportunity to spend some time with him and his wife. I knew Brother and Sister Jeffers operated in the gifts of the Spirit and I wanted to talk to them about ministry, specifically mine. When I met Brother and Sister Jeffers, they lived up to their reputations. The Lord showed them my life, the struggles, pains and shame. My heart broke when Sister Jeffers told me, "The rage and anger you grew up with nearly destroyed you. Did you ever wonder why God allowed it to happen? He could've stopped it but He allowed it. Do you know why?" While I was still thinking about her question, Brother Jeffers answered it for me, "It's because of what you do now, and what He has planned for you still." I had been talking to the Lord about my ministry, but the Lord wanted to talk to me about me. I knew I was being restored, strongholds were being torn down and healing was moving in me. Over the next year I was ridiculed, criticized, told I couldn't relate to this generation, that I lived in the past and didn't understand the times. In the past I would have found a way to let everyone know I was unhappy and being mistreated, but the Lord had prepared me for whatever came my way. He used the situation I was in to move me into a new ministry, one I had never really considered before. At first I thought it was a new call, but looking back I think that it was His plan all along. It just took a lot of time for me to be able to step into His plan. Because of God's immeasurable and enduring love, my wife and I have begun a "New Work" in my hometown.

Decades after becoming an ordained minister, I can finally say that I have learned to fully accept God's forgiveness and grace. I have come to know Him as my loving Father who loves me regardless of my past. I know that the failures of my past, anxieties about the present and fears for my future are all conquered by a loving Father who knows what we need before we even ask. I am witness to the wonderful, saving grace of Jesus Christ.

Edgar & Daisy Arias

2017 Automobile Accident

CHAPTER 9

Daisy & Edgar Arias

On Saturday June 24, 2017, the youth group that my wife and I (Edgar) teach had an event called "Encounter with Parents." We participated in activities that would help them improve their relationships. That Saturday, God put in our hearts to talk about "time" and how we should take advantage of it. Daisy showed them an hourglass that made them realize that we have only so much time to live. Just like this clock, our time is going by and eventually will come to an end. I stood in front of them and told them to close their eyes and imagine they were in front of God. God would ask them this question, "If you had twenty-four hours left to live, what would you do with your time?" Everyone answered pretty much the same. They would spend time with their family, showing them love and affection, asking forgiveness, repenting and putting themselves on good terms with God. I never imagined a short time later I too would have to respond to that question.

Four days later I (Daisy) met God face to face. The Lord gave me the privilege of visiting heaven and it was beautiful. Never in my wildest imagination had I seen something so glorious. The moment He spoke to me my life changed forever. I had a beautiful, supernatural encounter with God that I would like to share.

My husband, Edgar and I just finished breakfast and were getting ready to go to work. It was a normal morning and the weather outside was nice. Since my husband and I worked together, that morning I decided to take the wheel. It was a long, forty-five-minute drive and we always took the same route. It is a two-lane freeway, with no median barrier. The speed limit is fifty-five miles per hour and traffic is usually very light. We had been taking the same path to work and nothing had happened before, but today was a completely different story. By not reacting quickly enough, and somewhat panic-stricken, I tried to swerve out of the way of an oncoming car that was driving in our lane at sixty miles an hour, but the other car hit us head-on. It happened so fast that before I could catch my breath, we had made contact with the oncoming car. The crash was so powerful that our vehicle started spinning. Thank God, my husband and I had our seatbelts on. Since we were in the process of moving, the car was full of household things. In the back seat we had a plastic container full of books, games and dozens of DVDs. The impact was so strong that the whole front of the car, including the motor, smashed into the inside of the vehicle, crushing me between the car seat and the steering wheel. I was stuck and the impact left me unconscious.

Finally, the car came to a stop. I (Edgar) felt stuck; I couldn't move and started to feel pain in my right shoulder. I turned to the side and saw that my wife was unconscious. For some reason, she was breathing heavily and whimpering, but she was unconscious. I was relieved that at least she was making some kind of sound and was breathing. I knew she was alive. Knowing that if she didn't wake up and stopped breathing she would die, I started shaking her head and yelling at her, "Babe wake up, wake up," thinking that if I could keep her breathing until the ambulance arrived, it would be a good thing. I would then let the paramedics take over. While shaking my wife's head and yelling, suddenly, God spoke to me. He asked me many questions and gave me revelations, as if He was giving me the answers to life and the purpose of life. All the revelations connected with each other and everything made sense. All the questions God asked me started with "What if?"

- What if you do not become the person you want to become?
- What if you do not fulfill your goals? And many more, but the question that struck me the most was this:

- "What if I wouldn't have given you the opportunity to open your eyes once again, where would your soul have gone?"

Surprised by the question God had just asked, I began to reflect on the question and the reality of it. What if God did not give me the opportunity to open my eyes once more, where would my soul have gone?

More and more smoke started coming out of the car and it was getting very hot inside. I (Edgar) was waiting for the car to explode any second now. I closed my eyes and began to pray. I started repenting of my sins, asking for forgiveness and putting myself on good terms with God. I also began to express my love and asking forgiveness to everyone who popped into my mind. I thought the car was going to explode, but I was not willing to get out of the car. Even if it exploded, I was committed to staying there with my wife. Then I started to say goodbye to my family, to my friends, and finally I said goodbye to my wife.

The heat inside the car and the feeling of being stuck made me so desperate. I tried to open the door to get some air but it did not want to open. I started kicking the door until it finally opened. A DVD fell in front of me, and it landed on the road. When I saw the movie on the ground, it felt like a bomb of revelation had just exploded in my face. God was confirming everything He had asked me barely a few minutes ago. I could not believe it. It was a Christian movie named "What if?" Speechless, I saw the DVD and noticed a question below the title. It said, "What if God gave you a second chance?" God was speaking to me, and that moment God had given me a second chance.

My wife's silence brought me back to reality. I turned around and I realized that she was not breathing anymore. Scared, I again started shaking her head furiously, and yelling at her at the top of my lungs. "Babe wake up, please wake up!" It didn't matter how much I shook her head or how loud I shouted, she did not respond. I shook her head more and more and shouted as loud as possible, and still nothing. It felt like an eternity but five minutes or so after, she suddenly took a deep breath. I was relieved, and it was one of the happiest moments seeing my wife come back to life. I was getting desperate, and the pain in my shoulder increased more and more. It felt as if I my shoulder was on fire from the inside out and the pain did not let me sit still.

That day I was wearing a hat that my sister had let me borrow. From so much moving around, the hat fell off my head and landed on my lap. I stared at the hat, and it brought peace to my heart. It felt as if all the pain, fear and worry had left me. It gave me a feeling that everything was going to be fine. God used the hat to speak to me once again. The word "Blessed" was stitched on the front of the hat. When I saw the word "Blessed," I heard God whispering in my right ear, "You are blessed, everything will be fine." Peace then found its way into my heart and I knew that everything would be okay.

About twenty minutes after the crash, Edgar said the ambulance and the firefighters arrived. The police officers took my husband out of the car in a plastic stretcher and rushed him to the hospital. He arrived there with a fractured back, fractured right ankle, three broken ribs, a collapsed lung and his right shoulder broken and dislocated. Since I (Daisy) was trapped between the car seat and the steering wheel, the firefighters had to break the door to be able to get me out of the car. I arrived at the hospital unconscious, and because of my serious critical condition they had to rush me into intensive care. I arrived with fractures on my right ankle, right arm and my back, a wound behind my head that required ten staples to close, and three broken ribs that had punctured a lung.

And worst of all, a traumatic brain injury. The strong impact caused my brain to bleed and a couple of brain cells to die. My brain wasn't functioning properly and because of this, my body was not breathing correctly. I was not getting enough oxygen into my brain, so the doctors had to connect me to an oxygen machine. The brain injury left me in an unresponsive, vegetative state and in a coma. The doctors did not know if I was going to survive. They told my family to prepare for the worst. While I was in the coma, the doctors had to put a feeding tube in my stomach in order for me to eat. As the days passed, my condition worsened. Out of nowhere, an infection started in my stomach where they had put the feeding tube. Unfortunately, these tragic events were unfolding right before my family's eyes, yet in the spiritual world it was a completely different story.

God gave me the privilege to visit heaven. I found myself in front of Him. He was beautiful, something I have never seen before. While He stood in front of me I could feel His warm, unconditional love. It was a sincere, genuine, incredible type of love that you don't experience here on earth. God took time and showed me that I had actually died in the car crash and took me to heaven. I also saw roads covered with gold. God's clothing was snow white and brilliant as well. God's face shined so brightly that it illuminated heaven entirely. This made it impossible for me to see the features of God's face, but in my spirit, I knew it was God.

While in heaven I would look down, and I could see my family gathered inside my hospital room. The moment God spoke to me it was a life-changing moment. The first thing He told me was, "The young people love the world more than me." After that He told me, "Not all the church loves me, seeks me or does my will." He then proceeded to show me several people from my church that truly love Him. Sadly, it wasn't the whole church.

Heaven is an amazing place, a holy place. I did not feel sadness, anger, fear or any type of negative emotion. I was completely at peace. I was able to feel and experience God's tremendous love. I was not able to touch God, but God expressed His love towards me, in a way that I could actually feel. He also took the time to tell me that He loved me. Why was it that God was giving me this incredible opportunity to visit heaven? I'm just a normal, imperfect person. Why did He choose me? At that moment, God gave me the greatest mission of my life.

He told me that the reason why He was going to let me live was to testify about His power and to warn everyone that He is coming soon. Right after that, God made a waving motion and I saw that God put something in me. At that specific moment I came back to life.

Two weeks later, I was still unconscious, in a coma, but miraculously twenty-one days later, I opened my eyes. That's when my whole world changed.

The first thing I saw was my husband, holding my hand. Since I suffered a brain injury I was confused, I didn't know where I was or the reason why I was there. The brain injury left me unable to speak properly, eat, walk or be independent. I also suffered memory loss that still to this day I'm working hard on recovering. After I came out of the coma, I had to attend physical and speech therapy. In order to relearn how to walk, talk, eat, shower, brush my teeth and basically learn everything, I had to dedicate myself to these therapies. The fractures in my body made it very hard to move around. In church I couldn't stand for a long time, because of the back injury, and the arm fracture made it very hard for me to lift my hands and praise God. My ankle made it impossible for me to dance for God. I was in complete disarray.

Before the accident, my life was anything but perfect. I was raised by a very strict man. I couldn't talk and eat at the same time and I was prohibited to leave the table until everything on my plate was gone. I couldn't get a break; everything I did was being watched and controlled as if I lived under a dictator. I had to be on my best behavior at all times. Living like this made me feel miserable, and on multiple occasions, I tried to commit suicide. At the young age of fourteen, because of my parents' divorce I had to leave everything I knew. My friends, my school and the town I called home was left behind. I became angry and annoyed to the point I became depressed. I tried searching for happiness at parties and going out on the weekends. On two different occasions, I almost got kidnapped. After those traumatic experiences, I became anxious to the point that I thought I was always in danger. I would lock myself in my room and wouldn't come out. I was a prisoner in my own home. At the age of sixteen, I met my wonderful husband, but I did not know God until the following year. In 2013, at the age of nineteen, I married him.

You could say that our marriage was anything but perfect. I brought with me that demanding, controlling, strict attitude that I learned from my step-father. I always wanted things to be in a certain order, and things to be done a certain way. I was a control freak and always wanted to wear the pants in my marriage. It made me feel at peace, but this attitude brought nothing but problems to our marriage. We also struggled with selfishness, jealousy, financial misunderstandings and argued constantly. We had trust and forgiveness issues. This led to intimacy issues because we didn't understand ourselves. Every attempt to communicate with each other ended up either in an argument or a fight. BUT, God had actually given us the understanding and wisdom to have a happy, loving, passionate, fulfilled marriage. It got to the point where we were able to eliminate most arguments and issues between us. We had victory over our problems and we were loving each other once again.

We were both happy and on track to a dream marriage when all of that changed the moment I opened my eyes. I came back to life with head trauma, causing me to forget plenty of things, including our love story. I confused my husband for my father. Worst of all, for some reason the brain injury brought back all of our issues, problems and misunderstandings we had battled with and already had victory over. Everything that we had learned before the car accident was undone. All the effort and time that we had invested in our marriage to make it work went out the window. My brain injury challenged my marriage in a way I was not prepared for. The brain injury had caused memory loss, and difficulty understanding and solving problems. It also required plenty of patience for those who communicated with me.

I did not understood why God was making us start all over again. "Why?" I would ask the Lord. I knew there was a purpose but, "What is that purpose?" God slowly started removing the blindfold from my eyes and started showing me that He was using the consequences of my brain injury to mold my character. My husband was also included in this process. I finally understood that after every dark, painful valley comes a hill full of blessings.

Because of my brain injury, I am very limited in many ways. Everything was out of my control and responsibility for my care was placed in my husband's hands. Not being able to be in control, God has taught me patience, and is challenging me to trust my husband in every way. He is becoming the man he needs to be, and I like the change. Before the accident, he was a selfish man. He would only worry about himself and my physical condition has taught him that it is not only about him anymore. Now he is the one that's a step ahead of me. He cleans, cooks and worries about what needs to be done. Now he is becoming the leader God wants him to be. By not being able to be in control, God has taught me to work on my patience, faith, my marriage, and trusting Him.

Slowly, God was unveiling the purpose of why all of this was happening to me. I prayed and remained strong through this difficult journey. I kept my faith and prayed to God to help me with my injuries, since they caused me plenty of pain and discomfort. It did not take long for God to respond.

Sunday, October 8, 2017, Evangelist George Pantages came to our church as a special guest. At the end of the message, he called to the altar those who wanted to be healed. Without thinking twice, with a strong, firm, gigantic leap of faith I got up from my seat and walked to the altar. This was my opportunity to receive my healing and I wasn't going to waste it. Once I made it to the altar, he asked me which part of my body needed healing. I simply replied, "My right ankle." He then started praying for healing. I was convinced that something incredible was going to happen. I was determined to receive my miracle. He prayed for all the pain to go away, and for God to heal and restore my right ankle. Suddenly, I jumped up and started praising and dancing for God. The pain had gone away, I couldn't stop worshipping, jumping for joy, and praising God because I couldn't do that before the prayer.

Something unbelievable happened the next day. I had a follow-up appointment with the specialist who was helping me with my ankle. The visit prior to that one, the doctor decided to X-ray it to see how my fracture was doing. I could clearly see a solid fracture across my ankle. This visit he decided to perform another X-ray and you won't believe what happened. The fracture on my ankle was completely gone. It had disappeared, and it was no longer visible and the doctor could not believe it. How could the fracture disappear completely, that fast? Speechless he stared at me and finally uttered this: "You are a walking miracle. God is definitely on your side." The fracture was gone and so was my pain.

As thankful as I was towards God and His amazing grace, He was not yet finished. Friday, February 2, 2017, I spoke with Evangelist Pantages over the phone and he decided to pray for healing on my right arm and lower back. He prayed for all the pain to go away. He then told me to bend down and to put pressure on my arm to see if the pain was still there. Miraculously, the pain had disappeared. I couldn't thank God enough for everything that He was doing. I closed my eyes and this inexplicable event took me back three years prior to a time where I was struggling with a very painful back injury. An injury that left me unable to walk, an injury where my husband would literally have to carry me wherever I needed to go. It was an injury that dumbfounded the doctors because they could not find the root where this sharp, needle-like pain in my lower back was coming from. The same way God had just healed my ankle, arm and back, three years ago was the same way He healed this unknown sharp pain in my lower back. I was overwhelmed by God's love and power and how He keeps on healing me and demonstrating that love. Not just that, but the way God is performing miracles in others as well. He also healed my husband from his back injury. I can't thank God enough.

Every fracture and physical pain in my body, God has healed. I still suffer from memory loss; I sometimes forget what I was going to say, and sometimes it is difficult to understand others. Many times, it's overwhelming and challenging trying to solve everyday life problems. Have you ever tried searching for Waldo, the little man dressed in a red and white striped long-sleeve shirt, and hat? Waldo, the little man from the "WHERE'S WALDO" books? That's exactly how the brain injury makes me feel, as if I have to completely focus and go into my mind and search for every specific piece of information I need in order to understand others or to problem-solve. Yes, this process is very overwhelming and takes plenty of energy away from me, but I don't say all of this so that you may feel sorry for me. I have learned that God will show you His incredible, power when you are going through that painful, dark valley. I say all of this so you won't lose faith in God.

Every struggle, every painful valley, there is a purpose. Just like Isaiah 64:8 says, we are the clay and He is our potter, and we are all the work of His hands. I tell you that every negative situation that you are going through, God uses it to mold our character and make us into His image. When you feel uncomfortable going through that painful, difficult situation, lift your hands up and pray for God's help. Your situation is just simply the potter molding the clay into something amazing, something incredible, something powerful, and best of all, something beautiful! My walk with God has improved tremendously. Experiencing the glory of God and His miracles made me realize that there is no other place I'd rather be than walking with God. Every single day, He uncovers and gives me a piece of this confusing puzzle I call life. He has helped me understand the real purpose of all of this.

The doctors told my family that there was a great chance that I wouldn't make it, but God had the last word. As 2 Corinthians 5:7 says, we live by faith and not by sight.

In the accident everything broke. In the trunk I (Edgar) had pots and weights that also broke. But there was one thing that did not break. It was the hourglass that my wife had showed to the parents a week prior to the accident. How was it possible that something fragile and delicate didn't break? Is God trying to tell us something? In this tragic accident there were three people involved. God gave two of them a second chance, but for the third person her time was up, and she passed away. Will you take advantage of your time or will you waste it? Think about it...

George Pantages Ministries

Books Available in English

George Pantages Ministries
Cell 512-785-6324
GEOPANJR@YAHOO.COM
GEORGEPANTAGES.COM

George Pantages Ministries

Libros Disponibles en Español

George Pantages Ministries
Cell 512-785-6324
GEOPANJR@YAHOO.COM
GEORGEPANTAGES.COM

www.ingramcontent.com/pod-product-compliance
Lightning Source LLC
LaVergne TN
LVHW051605070426
835507LV00021B/2780